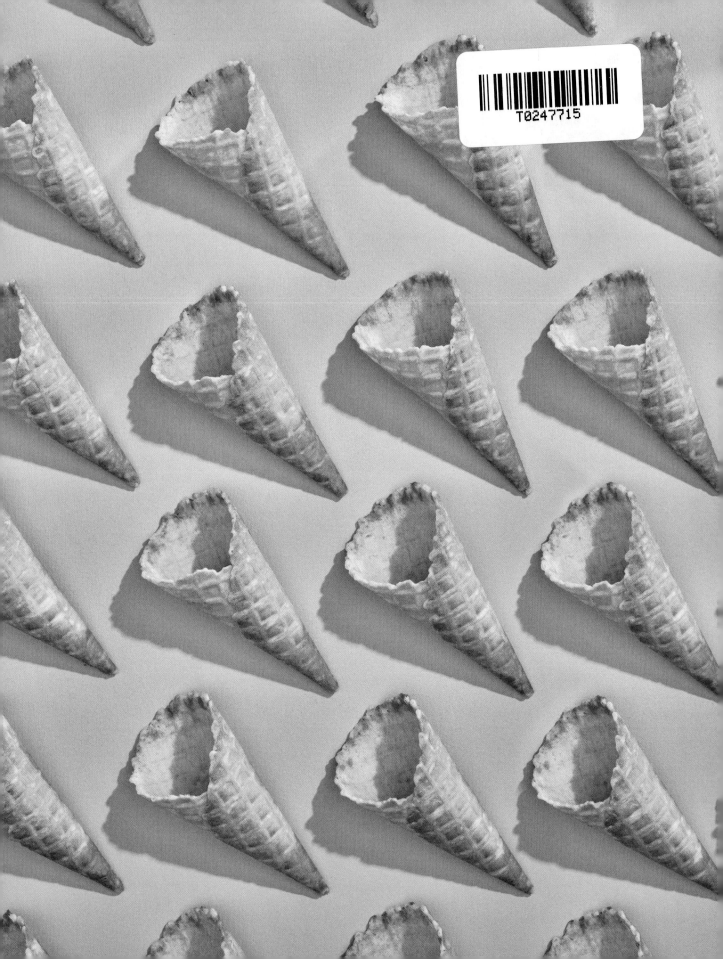

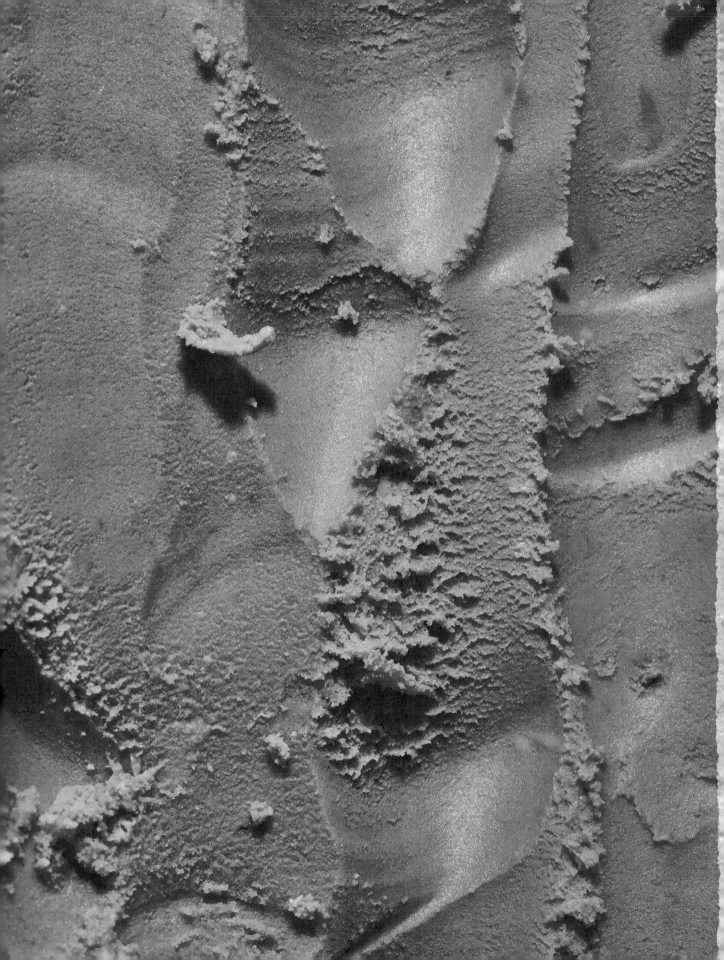

# GREAT SCOOPS

# RECIPES FROM A NEIGHBORHOOD

# GREAT SCOOPS

## ICE CREAM SHOP

MARLENE HALEY *and* AMELIA RYAN
*of* THE MERRY DAIRY
with ANNE DESBRISAY

**Figure.1**
*Vancouver / Toronto / Berkeley*

av. Fairmont Ave.
343 ← 102

This book is dedicated to everyone
who loves ice cream.

Cataloguing data is available from Library
and Archives Canada
ISBN 978-1-77327-165-1 (hbk.)

Design by Naomi MacDougall
Photography by Christian Lalonde,
Photoluxstudio.com
Prop styling by Irene Garavelli
Food styling by Noah Witenoff

Editing by Michelle Meade
Copy editing by Judy Phillips
Proofreading by Renate Preuss
Indexing by Iva Cheung

Printed and bound in Canada by Friesens
Distributed internationally by Publishers Group West

Figure 1 Publishing Inc.
Vancouver BC Canada
www.figure1publishing.com

# CONTENTS

# ICE CREAM FOR ALL

Can you imagine a life without ice cream? How empty it would be. Hot apple pie without à la mode. No midnight tub in bed to comfort a broken heart. Cones filled with nothing but air.

Science tells us that ice cream lights up the happy centres of our brain! (We hope they didn't spend too much money on that research.) After a decade of churning and scooping, we at The Merry Dairy can confirm what pretty much every lucky human knows from childhood: joy and ice cream are deliciously entwined. More than any other food, ice cream prompts happy-making memories ... of carefree summer days, of chasing the ice cream truck, of infinite fun with flavours and sauces and toppings, of sticky chins to wipe and fingers to lick.

Ice cream, at its most basic, is simple stuff—cream, milk, eggs, sugar. For centuries, before mass production, it was made in the home, hand-cranked over ice and rock salt, flavoured with raspberries from the garden, peaches from the orchard, rhubarb from the neighbour's patch. We want to bring that purity and ease of ice cream making back into the home—into *your* home, to fill your cones, to celebrate whatever needs celebrating in your lives—whether it's churned by hand (if that's still your pleasure) or eased along with some affordable mechanical help.

Ten years after that initial run in The Merry Dairy's first ice cream truck, we find ourselves still with our feet on the kitchen floor and our hands on the wheels, running a vibrant ice cream business with a merry team of churners and scoopers and bakers, all of whom have contributed to these pages.

It's with a sense of awe and gratitude for that decade of ice cream making that we present this book of recipes and stories.

MARLENE AND AMELIA

# HOW IT ALL BEGAN
## MARLENE'S STORY

Growing up on a farm, I never knew the thrill of that jingle—the "Pop Goes the Weasel" siren call to city kids everywhere that announced their day had just got a whole lot better. The ice cream truck was coming!

We didn't have ice cream trucks rolling down our rural road in southwestern Ontario. In fact, I didn't see my first such truck until I was in my late twenties, living in Manhattan with my husband, Bernie, in an apartment on West 89th Street. We had a school in front of us and another behind. And that's where I came to understand the meaning of those teasing tunes, played on an endless loop through the speakers of a slow-rolling lorry: it meant the music would be getting louder as the truck rumbled closer, and the happy-kid screams at the end of the school day would be deafening. As far as Manhattan noises went, it was a pretty good one.

The Haley family farm was in beautiful Brant County, nine miles outside the town of Brantford, not far from the city of Hamilton. I was the youngest of ten kids (eight girls, two boys) in a hard-working Irish Catholic family. A statue of the Virgin Mary adorned our front lawn, watching over family and farm. We milked eighty cows, raised chickens and ran an egg-grading operation. Milk, cream, eggs... pretty much our lives. So, you might suppose that homemade ice cream was a regular pleasure of my childhood, that the road from little-me back then on a dairy farm

to adult-me today, running an ice cream business, would be a pretty straight line. But the truth is, my mother was way too busy churning out meals and farm duties to be churning ice cream for me and my nine siblings. I'm not sure it even occurred to any of us to ask for the homemade stuff. We knew we could meet our friends at the Dairy Queen.

The Brantford Dairy Queen—now *that* was our idea of ice cream! For years, we'd pile into the family's Monte Carlo and head to Colborne Street, lining up with every other kid in town to order our faves—the Dilly Bar, the Curly Top, a Tripleberry Brownie Blizzard.

That awareness of ice cream shops as happy-making places, places that build community, has stayed with me, through an English degree in Ottawa, a master's at Columbia, a career in education and a decade of foreign-service postings with Bernie, a Canadian diplomat. It was likely why, after a few years' working contract to contract at various universities and colleges and mulling over options for doing something else, I settled on the idea of making gourmet ice cream and scooping it out of a truck.

A bit wacky, especially the truck idea, but the timing was perfect.

Our home was now Ottawa. The capital's food truck scene in the early 2010s was beginning to explode as the city loosened restrictions and granted a slew of licences. A truck, I figured, might be fun. And certainly

a lot less of a financial commitment than a bricks-and-mortar shop. Bernie was on board. Our two kids (then eleven and nine) were wildly keen. My mother, however, was a whole lot less into the idea. Growing up with parents who had lost everything in the Great Crash of 1929, she knew risk and loss. She knew poverty and despair. And I knew that her "Oh goodness, Marlene, don't give up teaching to drive a truck" grew out of understandable motherly anxiety.

My mom was not the only one with loving concern. I had friends who gently reminded me that Ottawa was just about the coldest city on the planet and that selling ice cream, at least profitably, could only work (if it worked at all) during our short summers. But it seemed to me it could be a sweet life: I would teach in the winter and churn ice cream in the summer. Besides, this was about more than the burgeoning food truck scene in Ottawa and some nostalgic imagining of the delight my ice cream truck might bring (all those smiling little faces!). This was a deep desire to introduce my city to frozen custard.

Because it was frozen custard, in fact, that truly changed my life, and probably planted the seed for what became a career in ice cream.

## FROZEN CUSTARD

So, just what *is* that stuff? In a nutshell, it's a dairy-rich dessert of cream, milk, sugar, egg yolks and flavouring. Truth is, I'd never met an ice cream I was wild about (Dairy Queen's included!) until I met a frozen custard. That meeting took place two decades ago on a sunny picnic bench somewhere in North Carolina on one of our many "Let's get outta Manhattan" road trips. We'd never travel without Bernie's bible: the Jane and Michael Stern book *Roadfood*, a guide on where to pull over for good grub. (Or, in our case, where to go miles out of our way for some lobster shack, a well-reviewed barbecue joint or a much-loved ice cream stand.)

That day, he'd read about something called "frozen custard." I remember not being much in the mood for whatever kind of ice cream that was. I told Bernie to help himself; I'd just take a coffee. But the guy came back with two cones. His, vanilla. Mine, the flavour of the day, pumpkin spice. I likely rolled my eyes, but that first taste was transformative. The feel of the ice cream in my mouth was so silky, so rich, so incredibly creamy and smooth and elegant. The texture was like nothing I'd tried before—almost chewy and certainly dense—and the taste was pure and clean. I was completely hooked. From then on, sourcing good frozen-custard places became a thing for us during our years in the States.

Later, back in Canada, I returned to teaching while also exploring my giddy new idea of scooping frozen custard from an ice cream truck in one of the freezing-est cities in the world. I researched types of trucks and scoured the internet for frozen-custard machines. I attended ice cream school in Missouri, studied ice cream making at the University of Guelph and flocked to ice cream conventions (truly, the happiest gatherings you'll ever attend). I did a ton of home-machine testing and started experimenting with flavours, making batch after batch of wild successes and awesome failures. I researched sources for the finest vanilla beans and chocolate, for local honeys and berries, teas and herbs. I talked to everyone I knew who knew anything about running a food truck or, even better, an actual ice cream truck. The latter didn't seem to exist. Sure, there were trucks selling colourful frozen confections, but none was serving a gourmet ice cream. And as for a nut-free gourmet ice cream, that did not exist. And that was the plan.

So, yes, it's a bit weird to be nut-free in the ice cream world—so many classic flavours contain them—but for us it made a world of good sense. Our son, Theo, has a peanut allergy. For him, and for some of his friends, the sheer joy of going out for ice cream was not an option. So, scooping ice cream that was safe for our family was a no-brainer; serving a guaranteed nut-free treat at school events, sports fields, fairs and playgrounds also made good business sense.

It all came together in the spring of 2012. I was feeling confident in my ice cream making. I'd sourced a frozen-custard machine from a small manufacturer in Michigan. And I'd found the truck of my dreams in a small town in Pennsylvania. The seller was Conrad Lern of Lern's Licks, a proud owner of a 1985 Grumman step van. He was particularly proud of its powerful generator, for which he'd done all the electrical himself (about which we were naively impressed). Shaking his head at our zany idea of using that generator for churning gourmet frozen custard, and in Canada of all places, he nevertheless agreed to remove his soft-serve machine and promised a parting gift of a CD playlist of all his precious jingles.

## A NOTE ON FROZEN CUSTARD

Frozen custard launched The Merry Dairy. It was our passion, back in 2012, to scoop it up from the American Midwest, bring it across the border to Canada's capital and introduce its many pleasures to our city via an ice cream truck. That was in 2012. The Merry Dairy is now merrier than ever. We've added more wheels, we've now a permanent shop with a proper production kitchen and we've grown our product line.

Frozen custard is still, and will always be, on offer at The Merry Dairy, but you won't find a recipe for making it in these pages. We've experimented with ways a home cook could replicate our frozen custard without using a commercial machine and, although the flavour of our attempts has been delicious, the texture isn't what we want. The silkiness of frozen custard relies on its rich custard base but also on the "continuous batch" barrel freezer that churns in a matter of minutes, with very little air in the mix. And that's what makes all the difference.

So, unless you happen to have such a freezer (or something like that), we invite you to enjoy fresh frozen custard at The Merry Dairy and use the recipes in this book to make our custard-based ice creams.

## LIFE ON THE ROAD

Just before the road trip down to the States to collect the truck, we'd finally settled on our name: The Merry Dairy. It was a Bernie idea, and one we all instantly loved. "Dairy" was for the connection to my farm roots; "merry" because it seemed a deliciously happy word, imbued with old-fashioned English mirth. And "merry" was also Bernie's cheeky nod to "Mary," the name my dear Catholic parents gave all eight of us Haley girls in one form or another.

It was Bernie and Theo who drove the ice cream truck home from Pennsylvania—a father-son road trip with Theo riding shotgun, being waved and honked at all the way north. Even the border guards were charmed, asking for a cone, giggling and waving them through—proving the capacity of ice cream to improve the mood of even the sternest of government officialdom.

The Lern's Licks truck's new home was at the end of our Ottawa driveway, now plastered with a monster "Coming Soon: The Merry Dairy" banner. Our daughter, Nadia, peeled off many decals; our mechanic certified the truck was in shape ("Well done. Great truck. These babies last forever."); we upgraded the generator's electrical to meet code ("Well, this was certainly MacGyvered together, lady."); and we painted the whole thing glossy white. The frozen-custard machine went in. We got a Twitter and Facebook account and created a QR code with a link to a site that included our (very limited) menu and an explanation of what the heck frozen custard is. This was all painted on the truck, next to the pretty pink double-scoop cones of our original logo. The "Free Wi-Fi" banner was also a brilliant thing. This was before everyone carried Wi-Fi around in their pockets. We just figured those drawn to our truck for its *gratis* surfing might fancy a cone while they browsed.

We were as ready as we were going to be. There was nothing left but to take our frozen custard to the people. I hit the streets on a sunny Saturday in June with a bucket of freshly made vanilla, two sauces and three toppings, announcing our location on Twitter (Stirling Avenue, Ottawa's self-proclaimed "hip strip"). I was beyond nervous. But it worked out famously. People were expecting us, and our music drew them out of their homes. The kids came flocking. I scooped for an hour and sold out.

As that first summer turned to fall and I returned to teaching full time, I felt that The Merry Dairy had landed. We had done end-of-school events (our nut-free product being a huge draw), a dog festival, a vintage car rally and many, *many* community and charity events. We'd received some lovely press, and our social media followers had blossomed to fantastic levels. Even my mother was getting excited.

A year later, it was time to make a choice. Trying to honour my teaching commitments and my mothering while spending evenings and weekends Merry-Dairy-ing was feeling like too much. Even managing Twitter, so brilliant for growing our business, was a part-time job. I was constantly updating the feed and responding to "Please come back!" requests from those watching our truck roll by, all the while trying to keep both eyes on the road. Truth is, I was feeling decidedly un-merry about it all. So the next spring I gave notice to my college and turned my full attention to ice cream. And to dreams of growing the business even more.

Fresh frozen custard is a delicious style of ice cream, but it has its limitations. I could make only one flavour at a time, so I had to rely on sauces and toppings to add interest and to mix things up. I started making ice cream sandwiches with extra custard, and those sold well. But daily I'd get requests: Can you make lemon? Can you make ginger? What about rum and raisin? Weddings were wonderful events for us, but the happy couple had their own ideas—there was that cone of mint chocolate chip on their first date. Could we make them some?

And people wanted to take our ice cream home, to their own freezers. But there was the rub: frozen custard is a fresh product. If it sits more than an hour or two, or gets stored in the freezer, it's no longer fresh frozen custard; it's parlour-style hard-scoop ice cream. Still delicious but not frozen custard. (See A Note on Frozen Custard sidebar, p. 11.)

Honouring these requests would require an expansion of our product line. Which meant we'd need a production kitchen with space for more equipment. One that was our own, not rented, not shared, and, most important, a space where we could ensure a nut-free environment. We wanted space to do all our own baking. We wanted to further our rallying cry of "Ice cream for all!" with a line of dairy-free ice creams and gluten-free cones, and we wanted to offer takeaway pints for home freezers and for other local shops to stock.

So many wants! But they all meant The Merry Dairy needed a home. Something that didn't have wheels. Something that would allow us to become a part of a community, to host fun events, to have real roots.

## HELLO, 102 FAIRMONT AVENUE

We found that home in the heart of Ottawa's Hintonburg neighbourhood. The building housing a long-running corner store, the Fairmont Confectionery, was for sale. Bernie and I knew the space well—and that it was perfect for us. In the spring of 2017, we launched the project of turning a century-old brick building with a host of other lives lived into the neighbourhood scoop shop of our dreams, and on the busy August civic holiday weekend, we opened our doors. It so happened to be my birthday. A very fine gift.

## ENTER AMELIA

Another very fine gift! This book would not exist without Amelia Ryan. The morning she knocked on the still-papered-up door of 102 Fairmont Avenue, resumé in hand, was the moment my ice cream business really heated up. Amelia came with a business degree and some serious baking chops. She also came with an abiding curiosity for understanding the art and science of ice cream making, and an enthusiasm for making customers' flavour dreams come true. Plus, she's a happy person, and that's a key ingredient in any ice cream venture.

## GROWING OUR FLEET

With our team and the business growing, it was time for more wheels. Our Merry Dairy "Mama" truck was joined by "Baby" truck (a vintage 1974 Grumman step van that had been a novelty truck on a beach in Long Island). The "Papa" truck came a year later, a bigger fellow with room for three of us to scoop, the perfect ride for high-volume events like festivals.

The Merry Dairy was expanding, but we stayed a scoop shop. We exist (and thrive) year-round, in a northern city with more winter than summer. And despite all those well-meaning folks and family who told us we'd need to supplement our frozen things with warming things from October to May—soup, say, and certainly coffee—we never have. The Merry Dairy serves ice cream. And that's that.

## A DECADE ON

The Merry Dairy has grown deep roots. We feel so incredibly lucky to be a part of a vibrant, supportive community, and we're grateful every day for our customers, young and old, on the road and in our 'hood. We see the joy ice cream brings, and we don't take the privilege of providing that for granted.

Joy is best when shared, so Amelia and I thought we'd like to do that. In these pages are our most delicious recipes, adapted for the home ice cream maker, along with easy strategies and tips for mastering technique, playing with flavour and churning up creativity. We at The Merry Dairy hope you scoop it all up!

## HOW TO USE THIS BOOK

Once you've established which ice cream machine you'll use (p. 16) and have a firm handle on making the ice cream base (p. 25 or p. 29), you're off to the races! Many of these recipes are straightforward; others require additional steps. Each recipe has been tested for the home churner on domestic ice cream machines by The Merry Dairy team, and by several keen helpers on their home machines, all eager to test and taste and to offer opinions and suggestions. You know who you are and we are grateful to you.

We wish you happy times with these recipes. They are meant to bring you and those you love great joy!

## WHAT, NO BUTTER PECAN?

From the get-go, The Merry Dairy was nut-free. This commitment came from the certain knowledge that our products—all of them—were going to be safe not only for Marlene's son, Theo, who is allergic to peanuts, but for all children. No kid would ever have to ask us about nut content, no parent would ever have to worry about trace contact and we'd never have to see despair on a little face as a kid turns away from our truck, their friends enjoying a treat they cannot eat. That was not going to happen.

In addition to our ice creams at The Merry Dairy being nut-free, they are also free of many other concerning allergens, including sesame, sulphites and, in most cases, wheat. For those who have plant-based diets, we offer vegan flavours. And our waffle cones (p. 209) are more than delicious—they're gluten-free (see Tip, p. 209) as well.

With that in mind, you'll find the following dietary symbols in the recipes, where applicable.

**GLUTEN**

**VEGAN**

# THE BASICS

Ice cream making doesn't require a big investment in time or equipment. Nor does it require a chemistry degree or years of cooking school. But since some grasp of the basic science of frozen treats is helpful, we've equipped you with that in these pages.

The rewards in artisanal ice cream making (beyond the obvious pleasure of consuming the end product) are found mostly in the small details. We've addressed all those throughout this book, including in a helpful Trouble-Scooping section (p. 210) of common errors explained and solved. That said, ice cream making can be mastered easily and, with attention to the basics and a bit of practice, you'll be a whiz in no time.

## WHICH MACHINE SHOULD I BUY?

There's no need to break the bank on a high-end machine in order to make great ice cream. In essence, the machine you buy will have two jobs: to freeze and to incorporate air into the custard by churning. Any one will do those jobs.

### ① ROCK SALT, ICE AND ELBOW GREASE

Actually, you don't need a machine if you're prepared to work up a sweat. Yes, you can buy hand-cranked or motorized machines of various sizes (wood, stainless steel or plastic). Or you can just do it yourself with a large bowl, whisk, bucket of ice and generous amount of rock salt. Burrow your bowl into the ice and salt (the salt lowers the freezing point of ice), pour in the custard and whisk until it starts to thicken. Once semi-frozen, place the bowl in the freezer for 10-20 minutes, then return to the ice bath to whisk for another 10 minutes or so. Enjoy as is, in a soft state, or freeze overnight for parlour-style hard-scooped ice cream.

This method requires the longest time of all the methods to freeze the ice cream base, and results aren't as consistent as they are with freezer bowls or built-in freezer machines, but rock salt, ice and elbow grease is the most affordable way to make ice cream.

## ❷ FREEZER BOWL

Before launching a flavour for large-scale production at The Merry Dairy, we test new batches in our two-quart Cuisinart freezer-bowl machine. These ice cream makers work by pre-freezing a double-walled bowl that, when inserted into the machine with a rotating paddle, churns and freezes the custard base as the internal coolant in the bowl thaws. The process takes about 20–40 minutes. There are fancier machines on the market, but we believe these freezer-bowl machines are light, easy to store and offer the best value. Since the bowl must be frozen between uses, you cannot make consecutive batches, but for about $100, the price is right. You could even buy two…

## ❸ COMPRESSOR MACHINE

These powerhouses make creating many batches of ice cream a breeze—and with no bowl to pre-freeze. An internal compressor cools the machine, churns and freezes the custard base and stops the churning automatically once it senses the ice cream is ready. It will also hold the finished product at a freezing temperature. While these machines make easy work of ice cream making, they have drawbacks—they are heavy, take up valuable counter space and can be quite expensive. Still, for making ice cream on a whim, or many flavours in a day, this is your machine.

# ICE CREAM AND BAKING TOOLS

Other than an ice cream maker (see pp. 16–17 for ideas on that), you don't need any specialty equipment to make ice cream. These are the tools we find useful—some of which we'd put in a "not essential but nice to have around" category. Most on this list you will find in any well-stocked home kitchen.

BLENDER  Useful in select recipes (Moscato-Poached Pear, p. 104) or in place of an immersion blender, but the best use for a blender is for whipping up a milkshake (p. 214)!

CANDY THERMOMETER  You can manage without a thermometer in ice cream making, but having a precise temperature readout takes a lot of guesswork out of knowing when the custard has reached the sweet spot of 180°F. Thermometers help enormously in knowing when thicker ice cream bases—such as Frosted Berry Tart (p. 66) or Triple Chocolate (p. 147)—have cooked completely, and they are critical for making sponge toffee for our Honeycomb ice cream (p. 100). We like instant-read digital thermometers best.

DISHERS  Not necessary but nice to have. Dishers have a trigger mechanism to release consistent portions of doughs, batters and truffles. They are a baker's secret to uniformly sized cookies. They come available in standardized sizes; we use #40 for our cookies.

FINE-MESH SIEVE  For catching any white bits of the eggs (the chalazae) and the flavourings (like a vanilla pod, tea leaves or cardamom pods) when pouring the hot custard into the ice bath.

FOOD PROCESSOR  Our sous chef. Makes easy work of tasks like chopping peaches (and catching their juices) for Ontario Peach ice cream (p. 86), puréeing roasted bananas for Banana Bread ice cream (p. 120), pulverizing cookies for ice cream cakes, and making bread crumbs for Buttered Toast & Jam (p. 178) ice cream.

ICE CREAM SCOOPS  Ice cream scoops, unlike dishers, are specifically designed for a frozen product. We use Zeroll brand scoops, which use the heat from your hand to gently warm the ice cream, making scooping a snap.

IMMERSION BLENDER  Also known as a hand blender. We use these handy tools to incorporate additions into ice cream bases.

KITCHEN TORCH  A blast to use—truly!—and the best way to torch marshmallows and toast meringue.

MEASURING CUPS, SPOONS AND KITCHEN SCALE  Digital scales are best for precise cooking and baking. Otherwise, use standard measuring cups and spoons for measuring dry ingredients and glass measuring cups for measuring liquids.

**PARCHMENT PAPER OR SILICONE MATS**
Parchment paper and/or silicone mats eliminate the need for greasing baking sheets, encourage even cooking and make rolling out sticky items a breeze. The paper can be manipulated to fit your pan exactly and reused many times before discarding.

**PASTRY BAG AND LARGE ROUND TIP**
For making our meringue kisses (p. 199) and profiteroles (p. 188), and for decorating ice cream desserts.

**PIZZELLE MAKER** Waffle cone and bowl makers are available to buy, but an inexpensive pizzelle maker will do the trick.

**OFFSET SPATULA** Useful for icing cakes and tarts, and for filling cakes with freshly churned ice cream.

**RASP/ZESTER** Also known by the brand name Microplane. We use rasps to zest citrus and grate whole nutmeg.

**STAND MIXER** We use a KitchenAid stand mixer, particularly handy for our baked goods (p. 199), our Snap, Merry, Pop ice cream (p. 46) and our Lemon Flapper Pie (p. 186).

**WAFFLE CONE ROLLER** An inexpensive cone-shaped tool used to roll homemade waffle cones, available in different sizes and from a number of suppliers. Or check YouTube for ways to fashion one DIY.

# PANTRY ESSENTIALS

We've divided the ingredients into two main types: those required to make the dairy and vegan ice cream bases, and those we use as flavourings and toppings.

### COCONUT MILK AND COCONUT CREAM

For the base of our vegan ice cream recipes (p. 29), we use cans of high-quality coconut milk. The brands we use (Aroy-D and Cha's Organics) contain only coconut and water and no other ingredients (such as stabilizers or emulsifiers; the latter won't allow the cream to separate from the milk). Our vegan recipes call for three cans of coconut milk, two of which are refrigerated to yield a rich coconut cream. When a can of coconut milk is chilled, the solid white mass of coconut cream (coconut fat) separates from the pale coconut water and rises to the top, allowing it to be scooped up easily.

There is a bewildering array of options for coconut products on market shelves. Avoid refrigerated "milk alternative," low-fat or "light" (aka "lite") coconut milk or sweetened products labelled "creamed coconut" or "cream of coconut." Many of these products contain additives that affect not only the clean flavour of the milk but also its ability to separate. So read the label before buying: the ingredient list should be very short!

CREAM  Heavy cream (sold as whipping cream in Canada) is typically 33–36% butterfat, one of the highest fat percentages in commercially sold dairy products. Fat is key! It's an essential component in making ice cream rich and, well, creamy, and the higher the fat content (we use 35%), the better. Cream is also a valuable carrier of flavour and a vessel for those flavours to bind to. It has properties that help make it resistant to curdling and to the formation of ice crystals. Fat also coats the palate, which means that if ice crystals did form, you are less likely to notice them. And finally, fat adds structure to ice cream that slows the rate of melting.

EGG YOLKS  Our dairy ice creams all start with a custard base, and custard starts with eggs. Specifically the yolks, which deliver a rich taste and creamy texture to ice creams. Egg yolks are natural emulsifiers, which means their proteins act on the sugar and dairy to enrich, to smooth and to prevent large ice crystals from forming. The added stability they deliver means the ice cream is less likely to melt too quickly; it also prolongs freezer life.

All the dairy ice creams and baking recipes in this book call for large eggs. We use the yolks for making ice cream, but egg whites keep well in the refrigerator and freezer. You'll find ideas for using them in the Tip on p. 199.

MILK  All the dairy ice cream recipes use whole milk (3.25% butterfat). Lesser-fat milks will work from a technical perspective, but the result will be a less creamy ice cream.

SALT  Salt is the silent hero backing any good ice cream. Salt knocks down bitterness and enhances and balances sweetness, sourness and umami tastes. You should not notice salt in your ice cream, but you will definitely notice its absence.

We use fine sea salt for all ice cream bases and for baking, and a flaky finishing salt when we want a pop of salinity and a nice bit of crunch.

SUGAR, WHITE AND BROWN  Granulated or white is likely the sugar you have in your pantry. Harvested sugar naturally contains molasses. When the molasses is expelled from the granules, you are left with sharp, white crystals that rarely cake together and dissolve easily into liquids or, in this case, into an ice cream base.

Refined brown sugar is white sugar that has molasses added back into it. We use brown sugar (light and dark) in ice cream and baking when we want a more complex and caramel flavour than would be achieved with white sugar.

## FLAVOURINGS

Flavourings are the building blocks that create the flavours we love! We do not compromise on their quality. We encourage you to pay attention to their provenance, buy the best you can afford and store them properly to protect their shelf life.

ACTIVATED COCONUT CHARCOAL POWDER  This incredibly fine, food-grade powder is made from burnt and ground coconut shells. We use it to dye the licorice ribbon in Tiger Tail (p. 96). Look for it at health-food stores or online.

ALCOHOL  If you've stored hard alcohol in your freezer, you know it doesn't really freeze. And alcohol's low freezing point matters when it comes to ice cream recipes: adding a glug will lower the freezing point, so the ice cream is softer and scoops like a dream, even if right out of the freezer. Add one too many glugs, though, and you'll ruin the integrity of the ice cream, meaning it will never fully freeze or will melt quickly into a goopy mess. Used in moderation, then, a couple of tablespoons of an alcohol like Cointreau, Chambord, kirsch or a cherry liqueur enhances fruit ice creams, while a premium brandy or rum works well with winter and autumn flavours.

ANNATTO  We use this peppery seed not for its flavour but for its vibrant colour. Even in small amounts, powdered annatto imparts a bright yellow-orange colour to ice cream. Native to Latin America, annatto can be found through spice vendors or markets specializing in Mexican and Latin ingredients—look for the powdered form.

CHOCOLATE AND COCOA High-quality chocolate is a pantry splurge but will make a world of difference to the flavour of your ice cream. A bar of chocolate should have a shiny surface, snap cleanly when broken, melt gently on the tongue and leave a pleasant lingering chocolate aftertaste. When hunting for vegan chocolate, look for a high-quality bar with cocoa of at least 70%. Without saying as much, many dark chocolate bars are vegan by default. The ingredient list of a vegan-friendly bar of chocolate should read: *cocoa, cocoa butter, sugar* and (sometimes) *soy lecithin* and *vanilla*.

For cocoa powder, use a high-quality unsweetened Dutch-processed cocoa, as it will incorporate more smoothly into ice cream bases than will natural cocoa. Cocoa has a natural tendency to clump, so when a recipe calls for sifting, please do so. When measuring by volume, use the same method as you would to measure flour: spoon (or sieve) cocoa into a cup without compressing, then level it off with a straight edge.

CITRUS JUICE AND ZEST Citrus brightens the palate and pairs beautifully with summer fruits. Zest citrus fruit before juicing it, and avoid the white pith. The juice of the fruit is usually added to the ice cream base ahead of the zest—read the recipe carefully!

COCONUT OIL Coconut oil is unique from other oils in that it is solid at room temperature. We use this property to our advantage when making chocolate freckles in flavours like Coffee with Chocolate Freckles (p. 171), Salt & Pepper Storm Chips (p. 166), and Peppermint Crackle (p. 148). When mixed with melted chocolate, the oil helps the chocolate harden upon hitting the cold ice cream. It also helps the chocolate melt in your mouth, even when frozen. We use unrefined virgin coconut oil.

COFFEE Coffee is clearly used in coffee ice cream (p. 138) but, like vanilla, coffee can also enhance other flavours, lending depth and complexity without leaving a detectable coffee flavour. We use both ground espresso beans and freeze-dried coffee (the highest-quality instant coffee available) in our recipes.

FLOWERS Edible flowers pair beautifully with ice cream. We use dried lavender buds for our Honey Lavender ice cream (p. 72) and buy dried hibiscus from our nearby Latin market (shoutout to Little Latin America on Somerset Street!) for Hibiscus & Passion Fruit ice cream (p. 45).

FRUIT In the winter months, we mostly use dried fruit like raisins and figs. But as soon as fresh local fruit is available, it becomes the driver behind many of our favourite ice cream flavours, sauces and toppings. The moisture in fresh fruit, however, can freeze into icy bits if not handled correctly. For ways to deal with that moisture, see Trouble-Scooping (p. 210). Note: Fruit sauces are better stored in glass containers than in plastic, which can affect flavour.

HERBS Fresh herbs brighten and add an earthy depth to ice cream. Mint, thyme, rosemary, basil—these can be tossed into the warm cream and allowed to steep. Tasting the cream as the herbs steep, before carrying on with the recipe, is the best way to judge when the strength of the flavour suits you.

HONEY We use honey from the Ottawa Valley—either Yellow House Honey from Richmond or Crerar's Honey from Vernon. Honey adds body to ice cream and tastes sweeter than regular sugar. Look for pure, unpasteurized liquid honey, and feel free to experiment with infused and local specialty honeys such as wildflower.

MAPLE SYRUP Maple syrup is graded into four colour classes, based on how much light is able to shine through syrup-filled glass bottles. Out of golden, amber, dark and very dark, we opt for the late harvest dark or very dark, for its potent maple flavour.

MOLASSES We use light, unsulphured molasses (pure sugarcane juice inverted into syrup) rather than the stronger blackstrap molasses, which we find too intense for our delicate ice creams.

SPICES To get a burst of cinnamon flavour in ice cream, we call for the powder; for subtle cinnamon notes, the full sticks. Always use fresh spices and freshly ground peppercorns.

TEA The best way to get a superb tea flavour is to use high-quality tea leaves. In these recipes, we use Sloane's Earl Grey tea for the Sugar-Plumped Fig & Earl Grey ice cream (p. 128) and a culinary-grade matcha for our vegan Matcha ice cream (p. 40).

VANILLA Earthy, exotic, wonderfully aromatic even in small amounts, vanilla is a flavouring agent in its own right and also an enhancer of other flavours (in much the same way as salt works in cooking).

At least the good stuff is. And it's the good stuff you must use. Wherever you source vanilla, make certain it is pure and from a reputable supplier. And yes, pure vanilla is expensive but its complex flavour and head-spinning fragrance are key to making quality ice cream. Look for plump, moist, pliable beans with a smooth surface and store them properly in a dark pantry to protect your investment.

We've spent many months experimenting with vanilla beans from various sources—Mexico, Tahiti, Indonesia, Uganda—but find that the sweet, creamy flavour of Madagascar beans, from the area formerly known as Bourbon Island (hence the name "Madagascar Bourbon vanilla"), suits us best.

## HOW TO SCRAPE THE SEEDS FROM A VANILLA BEAN

Using a sharp paring knife and leaving the curled top intact, slice the vanilla bean lengthwise down its centre, cutting only through the top of the bean. Use the dull edge of the paring knife to scrape the inside length of the bean, gently gathering the precious seeds. Warming the seeds and pod with the ice cream base coaxes out maximum flavour.

## REUSING A VANILLA POD

The mighty vanilla pod can be reused once it's scraped, as it will still impart flavour. Rinse off the cream and allow it to air-dry, then add it to a bowl of sugar (the resulting vanilla sugar can be used in our Ice Cream Profiteroles, p. 188) or salt, or drop it into a bottle of maple syrup for a gentle vanilla infusion.

# HOW TO MAKE
# OUR ICE CREAMS

Indulging in ice cream may be a spontaneous pleasure, but making ice cream requires some forethought. For one, the canister of a freezer-bowl ice cream maker (if this is the machine you are using) needs to be fully frozen to do its job properly, and this can take up to 24 hours. Even if you always store your canister in the freezer in anticipation of making ice cream (clever you!) or you're using a machine that doesn't require a frozen canister, the ice cream base still needs to chill in the refrigerator for at least 4 hours before churning—and we recommend even longer, for the flavours to develop. And if you want parlour-style hard-scoop ice cream, rather than the softer product that comes out of the canister, you will need to factor in a couple more hours of freezer time to further harden the ice cream.

So, with those caveats out of the way: Making ice cream is not difficult!

The base is the most unyielding part of the process. The set ratios of cream:milk:sugar (or coconut milk:coconut cream:sugar in the case of the vegan base) will ensure a rich, creamy, scoopable product, so we caution you to not stray from the recipe. Your creativity comes in the choice of flavouring agents—swap a grapefruit essence for lemon, add your favourite cupcake or square, play around with different teas, swirl in a homemade jam, or add a dash of cayenne pepper.

## EQUIPMENT

Ice cream machine (p. 16)

3-quart (2.75-litre) heavy-bottomed saucepan

Medium-sized bowl
(rubber-bottomed is useful
for stability, or place a damp
tea towel beneath it)

Whisk

Ladle

Heatproof spatula
(or flat-bottomed wooden spoon)

Fine-mesh sieve

Candy thermometer (recommended
for dairy ice cream, but not essential)

Ice bath

# MAKING A
# DAIRY ICE CREAM BASE

This is our master ice cream custard base, the starting point for every dairy-based ice cream in this book unless the recipe specifies otherwise.

2 cups (473 ml) heavy cream

1 cup (236 ml) whole milk

½ cup (100 g) sugar (or other sweetener, such as honey, pure maple syrup or molasses)

¼ tsp fine sea salt

**Optional flavouring agents (see recipes)**

5 large egg yolks (90 g) (See Tip p. 199 for ideas of what to do with the whites.)

## 1. PREPARE AN ICE BATH

Fill a large bowl (or your kitchen sink) with ice. Burrow a smaller bowl, preferably metal as it will cool faster, into the ice. Add cold water to the larger bowl just until the ice cubes are barely floating. (See photo on p. 29.)

*The job of an ice bath is to cool your ice cream base quickly, a job it performs faster than the refrigerator could. Cooling the base quickly halts the cooking process and lessens the chance of pathogens forming. So, yes, preparing an ice bath requires an extra step in the process of ice cream making, but it's an important one!*

## 2. WARM DAIRY AND SUGAR

In a heavy-bottomed saucepan over medium-high heat, stir together cream, milk, sugar (or other sweetener), salt and any flavouring agents the recipe calls for. Warm the mixture, stirring occasionally, until wisps of steam rise from the surface. (Be careful not to boil the mixture—it can quickly bubble up and cause a terrible mess.) Remove from heat.

## 3. TEMPER EGG YOLKS

While the dairy mixture is warming, whisk yolks in a bowl. Once the cream has reached temperature, arm yourself with a whisk in your dominant hand and a ladle in the other. Use the ladle to scoop up a small amount of the hot cream and add it in a thin stream to the yolks, whisking vigorously to prevent the eggs from scrambling. Continue whisking small amounts of cream into the yolk mixture until you've added about half of the cream. Pour the mixture into the saucepan.

4. **COOK THE CUSTARD AND STRAIN**

Cook the custard over medium heat, continuously scraping the bottom and sides of the saucepan with a heatproof spatula (or flat-bottomed wooden spoon) to avoid scorching. The custard is approaching doneness when it has visibly thickened, steam is rising off the surface and you feel a slight resistance when stirring. The custard is ready once you can draw a finger through it across the back of the spatula without the line filling in. If you're using a thermometer, it should read 180°F. Do not allow the mixture to heat beyond 180°F or you risk a curdled custard. Immediately remove the custard from the heat and strain through a fine-mesh sieve into the inner bowl of the prepared ice bath.

*Straining catches the eggs' chalazae, the white strands that suspend the yolk in the white, and any solid flavouring agents you've steeped in the cream.*

5. **COOL**

If desired, retrieve any flavouring agent (such as a vanilla bean) from the sieve and add to the cooling custard to intensify the flavour. Cool to room temperature, stirring occasionally.

6. **CHILL THE BASE**

Cover and chill the base for a minimum of 4 hours. All the bases at The Merry Dairy spend the night in our refrigerators, and we recommend that extra chilling time for yours too.

An unchurned ice cream base can be stored for up to 3 days in the refrigerator—or for up to 2 months in the freezer, then defrosted overnight in the refrigerator before churning and refreezing.

*Why chill? Just as a curry or chilli tastes better on its second day, a chilled-out base will become more interesting. The base will thicken a bit as it rests, and the fat in the dairy will bind with the emulsifiers in the egg yolks, resulting in a creamy, smooth ice cream.*

7. **CHURN/FREEZE**

Before churning, chill (in the freezer) the vessel you will use to store the ice cream. If the base is well chilled and the canister (if using a freezer-bowl machine) is fully frozen, you're ready to churn. Before adding the base to the canister, give it a taste: if the flavour needs a boost, fine-tune as you wish. Churning time depends on the machine; follow the manufacturer's instructions on how to churn and for how long, bearing in mind that the ice cream will seem soft even when it is fully churned. (See Churning Time, p. 28.)

8. **INCORPORATE ADD-INS, SWIRLS AND TOPPINGS**

**ADD-INS.** The best time to incorporate add-ins (bits of cookie, cake, brownie, tart or pie; shards of chocolate; crushed candy—whatever you fancy) is once the ice cream is completely churned. At this point, the ice cream will be thick enough to suspend the bits; they won't sink to the bottom but will be evenly distributed. Simply drop in the additions and let them incorporate for about 30 seconds before removing the finished ice cream from the machine. And although it goes without saying, we'll say it anyway: Anything you add will freeze in the ice cream. Make sure the inclusions are small enough that you, and your teeth, are happy encountering them in that state.

**SWIRLS.** Adding a swirl requires a little finesse and is best done as you transfer the ice cream to its (chilled) storage container. Spoon a few scoops of just-churned ice cream into the container, then dollop the jam, fruit sauce, caramel or chocolate sauce on top. Using a butter knife, gently swirl into the ice cream. Resist over-swirling. Repeat the process with another layer of ice cream and sauce, then freeze.

**TOPPINGS.** Here's where you can go wild! Load up your scoop with your heart's desire of toppings. See p. 34 for inspiration.

## STORING ICE CREAM

If you are not going to gobble down a quart of ice cream right after churning, use these tips for keeping ice cream fresh and ice-cap-free in the freezer.

**USE A WIDE, FLAT, AIRTIGHT CONTAINER, PREFERABLY PRECHILLED.** Ironically, the best storage vessel is not a standard pint tub. A wide container allows the ice cream to freeze faster, reducing ice formation. Find one that holds all the ice cream, with little head space left for air. Place a piece of parchment paper over the surface to minimize freezer burn further.

**GET IT BACK IN THE FREEZER.** The bane of any ice cream is melting and refreezing. Scoop what you want and get the rest back into the cold.

**STORE ICE CREAM IN THE COLDEST PART OF THE FREEZER.** That spot is not the door! The far back bottom is the most consistently cold spot in any freezer.

**EAT IT SOON.** Homemade ice cream is best enjoyed within 2 weeks of it being made.

## CHURNING TIME

The type and brand of machine, the size of bowl, the volume of the custard, the amount of sugar and alcohol, and the temperature of the custard all affect churning time. In other words, there are too many variables for us to give an exact time. Having said that, here are no-fail tells of perfectly churned ice cream:

The consistency looks like soft serve, thick and light.

The beater bars of the ice cream machine leave a trail in the semi-soft ice cream.

When a spoon is swiped along the top of the ice cream, it creates a deep valley without filling in.

The overall volume has increased by about a third.

NOTE: If a veneer of ice cream remains on the sides of the machine's canister, let it soften slightly, then eat—consider it a chef's reward.

# MAKING A VEGAN
# ICE CREAM BASE

Many vegan ice cream recipes begin with nut milks, such as cashew. As The Merry Dairy has a policy of nut-free, clearly ours could not. Still, we wanted a dairy-free ice cream that was rich, creamy and smooth, one with pure, clean flavours.

We opted for a coconut-milk base, a blend of coconut milk and coconut cream, and have come to love its versatility. Unlike cashew, coconut is not a neutral canvas. This allows us to play with it as a flavour in its own right, embracing it big-time in recipes like our Toasted Coconut (p. 42), while allowing it to be a gentle presence in Piña Colada (p. 156). Or, we might have it completely disappear (even those who are anti-coconut find it undetectable in our Peppermint Crackle, p. 148). Make sure you buy high-quality coconut milk that is free of stabilizers and other additives. The ingredient list should list only two: coconut and water. (See more on this in Pantry Essentials, p. 20.)

The vegan ice cream recipes in the book are astonishingly easy to make: ingredients are tossed into a saucepan and heated until the solids and sugars are dissolved and the chosen flavouring has sufficiently infused. No tempering required!

2 (400 ml) cans coconut milk, chilled for 24 hours

1 (400 ml) can coconut milk, room temperature

1½ cups (300 g) sugar (or other sweetener such as pure maple syrup or molasses)

¼ tsp fine sea salt

Optional flavouring agents (see recipes)

1.  **PREPARE AN ICE BATH**

    Fill a large bowl (or your kitchen sink) with ice. Burrow a smaller bowl, preferably metal as it will cool faster, into the ice. Add cold water to the larger bowl just until the ice cubes are barely floating.

    *The job of an ice bath is to cool your ice cream base quickly, a job it performs faster than the refrigerator could. Cooling the base quickly halts the cooking process and lessens the chance of pathogens forming. So, yes, preparing an ice bath requires an extra step in the process of ice cream making, but it's an important one!*

2.  **WARM COCONUT AND SUGAR, THEN STRAIN**

    Scoop out 1½ cups (350 g) coconut cream from the chilled cans of coconut milk (see p. 30). In a medium-sized saucepan, whisk together coconut cream, coconut milk, sugar (or other sweetener), salt and any flavouring agents the recipe calls for. Stir over medium-high heat for 5–7 minutes, until sugar is dissolved and no visible bits of coconut cream remain. Remove from heat and strain through a fine-mesh sieve into the inner bowl of the prepared ice bath.

## HOW TO EXTRACT COCONUT CREAM FROM CANNED COCONUT MILK

To extract the coconut cream from the milk, chill the cans of coconut milk in the refrigerator for at least 24 hours. Once chilled, the cream will have separated from the coconut water and risen to the top of the cans. It is this cream that you'll scoop out to use in the recipes. Depending on the brand of coconut milk, the fat will be either a silky cream or a solid mass. Both are great.

We often use the leftover coconut water in a smoothie, or for cooking rice or oatmeal. And sometimes for watering plants!

3. **COOL**

   If desired, retrieve any flavouring agent (such as a vanilla pod) from the sieve and add to the cooling custard to intensify the flavour. Cool to room temperature, stirring occasionally.

4. **CHILL THE BASE**

   Cover and chill the base in the refrigerator for a minimum of 4 hours, though longer is better to allow the base to thicken and the flavour to deepen. If a layer of solids has formed on the top of the chilled base, not to worry. We're all about the fat! Give it all a quick mix to incorporate before churning.

   An unchurned ice cream base can be stored for up to 3 days in the refrigerator—or for up to 2 months in the freezer, then defrosted overnight in the refrigerator before churning and refreezing.

   *Why chill? Just as a curry or chilli tastes better on its second day, a chilled-out base will become more interesting. The base will thicken a bit as it rests, and the fat in the dairy will bind with the emulsifiers in the egg yolks, resulting in a creamy, smooth ice cream.*

5. **CHURN/FREEZE**

   If the base is well chilled and the canister (if using a freezer-bowl machine) is fully frozen, you're ready to churn. Before adding the base to the canister, give it a taste: if the flavour needs a boost, fine-tune as you wish. Churning time depends on the machine; follow the manufacturer's instructions on how to churn and for how long, bearing in mind that the ice cream will seem soft even when it is fully churned. (See Churning Time, p. 28.)

   The vegan base is ready when (with the machine turned off) you can scoop a big spoon of it and then watch the ice cream fall back into the bowl in thick trails. If the scooped ice cream sits on top of the remaining ice cream in the canister before slowly incorporating, it's ready. If the ice cream incorporates right away, churn/freeze for another 3–5 minutes.

   NOTE: Even when churned to perfection, vegan ice cream will not be as frozen as its dairy counterpart. Look for the indicators listed in the p. 28 sidebar, but do not be concerned if the ice cream is softer than soft serve, with a consistency of loose pudding.

6. **INCORPORATE ADD-INS, SWIRLS AND TOPPINGS**

   **ADD-INS.** The best time to incorporate add-ins (bits of cookie, cake, brownie, tart or pie; shards of chocolate; crushed candy—whatever you fancy) is once the ice cream is completely churned. At this point, the ice cream will be thick enough to suspend the bits; they won't sink to the bottom but will be evenly distributed. Simply drop in the additions and let them incorporate for about 30 seconds before removing the finished ice cream from the machine. And although it goes without saying, we'll say it anyway: Anything you add will freeze in the ice cream. Make sure the inclusions are small enough that you, and your teeth, are happy encountering them in that state.

   **SWIRLS.** Adding a swirl requires a little finesse and is best done as you transfer the ice cream to its (chilled) storage container. Spoon a few scoops of just-churned ice cream into the container, then dollop the jam, fruit sauce, caramel or chocolate sauce on top. Using a butter knife, gently swirl into the ice cream. Resist over-swirling. Repeat the process with another layer of ice cream and sauce, then freeze.

   **TOPPINGS.** Here's where you can go wild! Load up your scoop with your heart's desire of toppings. See p. 34 for inspiration.

# THE CREATIVE PROCESS

The seasons are a driving force in the development of our flavours. As seasons change, particularly the long winter to spring, we find renewed energy in the kitchen: the rhubarb patch is ready to harvest! Raspberries are flooding the markets, and here come Ontario peaches, sweet corn, dark cherries, late plums and autumn pears. We'll make apple pies and toss them in our ice creams! And soon our fields are lumpy with bright orange pumpkins and squash, and we start toasting all those fragrant Thanksgiving spices. The winter holiday season has us plumping figs, juicing ginger, crushing candy canes, toasting oak chips and reaching for the whiskey bottle. For our ice creams, we mean.

But while the seasons and holidays are key motivators, our flavours are also created by our customers. "Can you make...?" is a daily question from those seeking a taste of nostalgia—the rum and raisin of their Trinidadian childhood (with "proper Caribbean rum"); the honey ice cream they remember their beekeeping grandfather made; the amazing spiced chocolate ice cream they had on a beach in Mexico. Kids generally want sweet ice creams filled with treats, and we've complied with add-ins of homemade cookies (p. 84), toaster tarts (p. 66), Rice Krispie treats (p. 46) and caramel popcorn (p. 136).

Ice cream also provides us with an opportunity to be inventive, to take a traditional flavour (rhubarb, say) and kick it up a notch (p. 56); to create an ice cream to celebrate a quintessentially Canadian event, the Snow Day (p. 160); or sometimes just to get a laugh (p. 60).

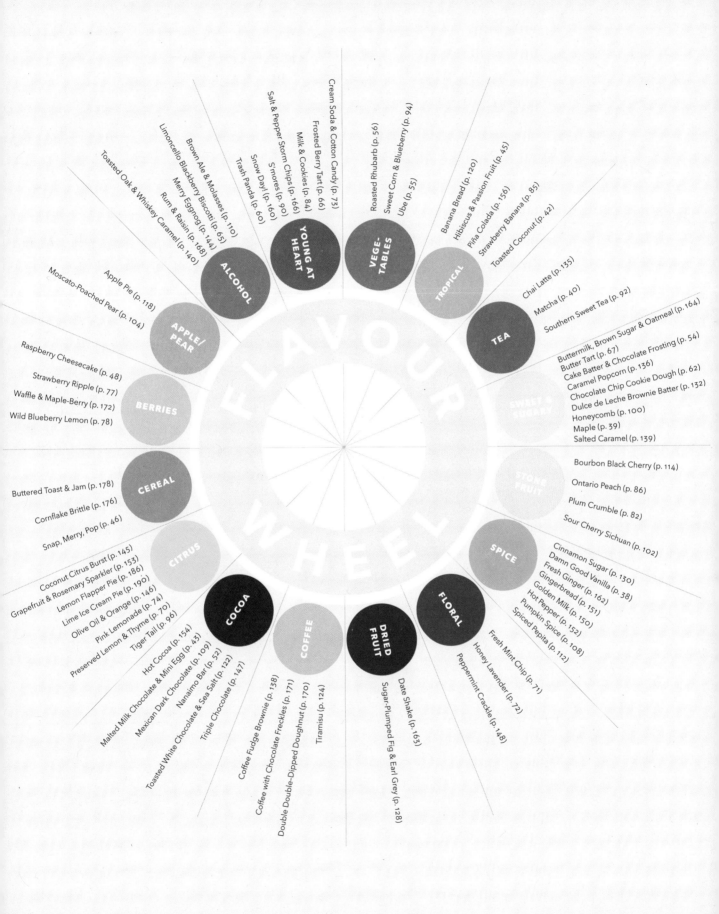

# FLAVOUR WHEEL

**YOUNG AT HEART**
- Cream Soda & Cotton Candy (p. 73)
- Frosted Berry Tart (p. 66)
- Milk & Cookies (p. 84)
- S'mores (p. 90)
- Snow Day! (p. 160)
- Trash Panda (p. 60)
- Salt & Pepper Storm Chips (p. 166)

**ALCOHOL**
- Brown Ale & Molasses (p. 110)
- Limoncello Blackberry Biscotti (p. 65)
- Merry Eggnog (p. 144)
- Rum & Raisin (p. 168)
- Toasted Oak & Whiskey Caramel (p. 140)

**VEGE-TABLES**
- Roasted Rhubarb (p. 56)
- Sweet Corn & Blueberry (p. 94)
- Ube (p. 55)

**TROPICAL**
- Banana Bread (p. 120)
- Hibiscus & Passion Fruit (p. 45)
- Piña Colada (p. 156)
- Strawberry Banana (p. 85)
- Toasted Coconut (p. 42)

**TEA**
- Chai Latte (p. 135)
- Matcha (p. 40)
- Southern Sweet Tea (p. 92)

**APPLE/PEAR**
- Apple Pie (p. 118)
- Moscato-Poached Pear (p. 104)

**BERRIES**
- Raspberry Cheesecake (p. 48)
- Strawberry Ripple (p. 77)
- Waffle & Maple-Berry (p. 172)
- Wild Blueberry Lemon (p. 78)

**SWEET & SUGARY**
- Buttermilk, Brown Sugar & Oatmeal (p. 164)
- Butter Tart (p. 67)
- Cake Batter & Chocolate Frosting (p. 54)
- Caramel Popcorn (p. 136)
- Chocolate Chip Cookie Dough (p. 62)
- Dulce de Leche Brownie Batter (p. 132)
- Honeycomb (p. 100)
- Maple (p. 39)
- Salted Caramel (p. 139)

**CEREAL**
- Buttered Toast & Jam (p. 178)
- Cornflake Brittle (p. 176)
- Snap, Merry, Pop (p. 46)

**STONE FRUIT**
- Bourbon Black Cherry (p. 114)
- Ontario Peach (p. 86)
- Plum Crumble (p. 82)
- Sour Cherry Sichuan (p. 102)

**CITRUS**
- Coconut Citrus Burst (p. 145)
- Grapefruit & Rosemary Sparkler (p. 153)
- Lemon Flapper Pie (p. 186)
- Lime Ice Cream Pie (p. 190)
- Olive Oil & Orange (p. 146)
- Pink Lemonade (p. 74)
- Preserved Lemon & Thyme (p. 70)
- Tiger Tail (p. 96)

**SPICE**
- Cinnamon Sugar (p. 130)
- Damn Good Vanilla (p. 38)
- Fresh Ginger (p. 162)
- Gingerbread (p. 151)
- Golden Milk (p. 150)
- Hot Pepper (p. 152)
- Pumpkin Spice (p. 108)
- Spiced Pepita (p. 112)

**COCOA**
- Hot Cocoa (p. 154)
- Malted Milk Chocolate & Mini Egg (p. 43)
- Mexican Dark Chocolate (p. 109)
- Nanaimo Bar (p. 52)
- Toasted White Chocolate & Sea Salt (p. 122)
- Triple Chocolate (p. 147)

**COFFEE**
- Coffee Fudge Brownie (p. 138)
- Coffee with Chocolate Freckles (p. 171)
- Double Double-Dipped Doughnut (p. 170)
- Tiramisu (p. 124)

**DRIED FRUIT**
- Date Shake (p. 163)
- Sugar-Plumped Fig & Earl Grey (p. 128)

**FLORAL**
- Fresh Mint Chip (p. 71)
- Honey Lavender (p. 72)
- Peppermint Crackle (p. 148)

# BEST SERVED COLD
## BUILD YOUR OWN ICE CREAM

We hope you enjoy our ice creams as much as we enjoy making them for you. DIY ice cream is so much fun, and we love creating new flavours to reflect the seasons, novel ingredients and requests made by our customers. And once you feel confident enough with the process, we imagine you'll want to do the same. It's a great way to exercise creativity—and feel a sense of accomplishment in making a winning flavour combination. (The flavour possibilities are endless, so dare to experiment.)

A caveat: Some of our favourite flavourings can really impact the final product. For example, sugar and alcohol lower the freezing point of ice cream (p. 211), and brewed coffee, tea and fruit can add too much water, resulting in ice (p. 213). We've provided you with a safe starting point, along with suggested add-ins, swirls and toppings to guarantee flavour success.

**1** **Choose a Base Recipe**

Banana (p. 85)

Cheesecake (p. 48)

Chocolate (pg. 147)

Coffee (p. 138)

Damn Good Vanilla (p. 38)

Dulce de Leche (p. 132)

Honey (p. 100)

Lemon (p. 186)

Lime (p. 190)

Maple (p. 39)

Olive Oil (p. 146)

Peppermint (p. 148)

Salted Caramel (p. 139)

Strawberry (p. 77)

Toasted Coconut (p. 42)

## Added Cool: Add-ins (½ cup)

Add-ins are the perfect opportunity to use up various leftover treats. Simply drop the additions into the base and let them incorporate for 30 seconds before removing the finished product from the machine. Favourite off-menu add-ins include fresh herbs, malt balls, candied jalapeños, poppyseeds, granola clusters, butterscotch chips, and candied bacon.

The ideal time to add in cookies, brownies and other treats is when the ice cream is fully churned. Add-ins should be room temperature, chilled or frozen—not hot—when added. And remember, you want to make sure they are small enough that you, and your teeth, are happy encountering them in that state.

## Give It a Swirl! (¼–½ cup)

Adding a swirl to ice cream can boost both the taste and the look, and options for swirling are many: any of our sauces (pp. 196–98) would work, or your own homemade jam. Try a swirl of lemon curd in a cheesecake base, or raspberry sauce in a chocolate base.

Swirls are best added when transferring the ice cream to the storage container. Spoon a few scoops of just-churned ice cream into your container. Dollop on your favourite sauce and, using a butter knife, gently swirl it into the ice cream. Over-swirling will muddle the swirl. Repeat by layering with ice cream and your swirl of choice. See the sauce chapter (p. 196) for more inspiration!

## Level Up: Toppings (½ cup)

Toppings are where you can really go to town! Consider using ingredients that pair well with ice cream but either don't freeze well (fresh, untreated fruit) or turn into frozen bullets (hard candy, say). All our sauces work well as ice cream toppings and can act as the sticky security for loose bits of another topping. Try any of these for toppings: balsamic vinegar and fresh strawberries, a shot of espresso, olive oil and fresh basil, wasabi peas, chocolate sauce and chili powder, edible flowers, pomegranate molasses, torched meringue, brandied cherries, caramel corn.

## THE MERRY DAIRY MASH-UP

In the spirit of creating, take your wildest idea and make it into a flavour. Here are a few of our fun mash-ups—flavours that recreate a memory, a favourite treat or just a great combination. There are countless flavour-mashes to be discovered, so experiment and make it weird!

**ARNOLD PALMER**
Earl Grey base (p. 128) + lemon zest (mix in after straining) + Lemon Curd (p. 197) swirl

**TERRY'S CHOCOLATE ORANGE**
Chocolate base (p. 147) + 3 Tbsp (18 g) packed navel orange zest (mix in after straining)

**CHERRY CHIP**
Damn Good Vanilla (p. 38) + mini chocolate chips add-in + Sour Cherry Compote (p. 102) swirl

**CAMPFIRE**
S'mores (p. 90) + a few drops of liquid smoke (mix in after straining)

**FUNFETTI**
Damn Good Vanilla (p. 38) + rainbow sprinkles add-in

**LEMON & RHUBARB**
Lemon base (p. 186) + Roasted Rhubarb Purée (p. 57) swirl

**PEACH BELLINI**
Ontario Peach (p. 86) + 3 Tbsp (45 ml) sparkling wine (mixed in after straining)

**STRAWBERRY TOASTED COCONUT**
Toasted Coconut (p. 42) + Strawberry Sauce (p. 196) swirl

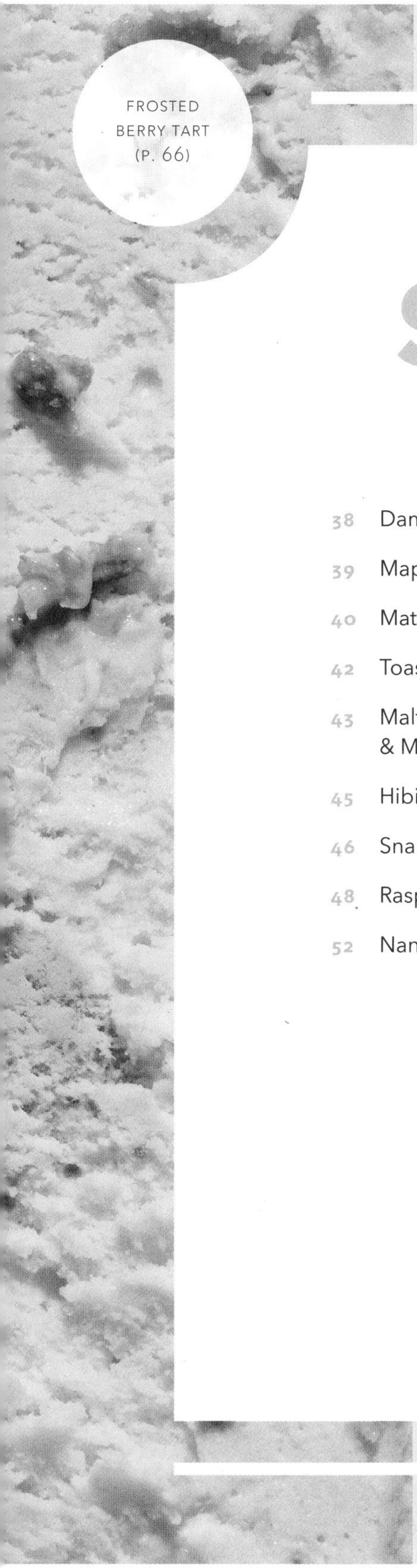

FROSTED
BERRY TART
(P. 66)

# SPRING

The mother of all ice creams. Vanilla is magnificent as a flavour in its own right but also the perfect blank canvas you can glam up in all manner of ways. It is the flavour that launched The Merry Dairy, and it remains still damn good and our number one seller. What to serve with vanilla ice cream is more a question of what *not* to serve with it. We are particularly partial to topping a scoop or two with lemon curd (p. 197) or using it as filling in ice cream sandwiches made with Ginger Molasses Cookies (p. 200) or Salted Oatmeal Chocolate Chip Cookies (p. 201). And it's perfect with a warm Butter Tart (p. 204).

# DAMN GOOD VANILLA

MAKES ABOUT 1 QUART

1. Prepare an ice bath (p. 25).

2. In a heavy-bottomed saucepan, combine cream, milk, sugar and salt. Scrape seeds from the split vanilla bean (see Tip, p. 23) and add the seeds along with its scraped pod into the saucepan. Stir over medium high heat for about 5 minutes, until steam begins to rise from the surface. Remove from heat.

3. While dairy is warming, whisk egg yolks in a medium-sized bowl. To temper the yolks, slowly pour 1 cup of the heated cream mixture into the yolks while whisking vigorously. Continue adding heated cream little by little and whisking until about half of the hot cream has been added. Transfer the yolk mixture to the saucepan.

4. Cook the mixture over medium heat, stirring continuously with a heatproof spatula, until the mixture is thick enough to coat the spatula or a digital thermometer reads 180°F (about 5–6 minutes). Immediately remove from heat and strain the custard through a fine-mesh sieve into the inner bowl of the prepared ice bath.

5. Stir in vanilla extract. Add the vanilla pod back into the custard to intensify the vanilla flavour. Cool the custard in the ice bath until room temperature, stirring occasionally. Cover and chill in the refrigerator for at least 4 hours, or overnight.

6. Remove vanilla pod (see Tip on p. 23 for reusing it). Place storage container in the freezer to chill. Freeze the mixture in an ice cream maker according to the manufacturer's instructions, until ice cream is thick and creamy and has increased in volume by about a third.

7. Enjoy immediately or freeze 2 hours in chilled storage container for a firmer scoop. For storage tips see p. 28.

2 cups (473 ml) heavy cream

1 cup (236 ml) whole milk

½ cup (100 g) sugar

¼ tsp fine sea salt

1 (4-inch) vanilla bean, cut lengthwise

5 large egg yolks (90 g)

½ tsp pure vanilla extract

Maple syrup makes life so much sweeter, and we are lucky to be surrounded by top-notch maple syrup farmers, including the fifth-generation Coutts family, in the Ottawa Valley. Their syrup arrives at our door freshly boiled, with a bold flavour and a rich, dark colour. As a nut-free shop, we don't have maple walnut ice cream, but nothing's stopping you from tossing candied walnuts into this ice cream at home.

# MAPLE

MAKES ABOUT 1 QUART

1. Prepare an ice bath (p. 25).

2. In a medium-sized saucepan, combine cream, milk, maple syrup and salt. Stir over medium-high heat for about 5 minutes, until steam begins to rise from the surface. Remove from heat.

3. While the dairy is warming, whisk the egg yolks in a medium-sized bowl. To temper the yolks, slowly pour 1 cup of the heated cream mixture into the yolks while whisking vigorously. Continue adding heated cream and whisking until about half of the hot cream has been added. Transfer the yolk mixture to the pan.

4. Cook the mixture over medium heat, stirring continuously with a heatproof spatula, until the mixture is thick enough to coat the spatula or a digital thermometer reads 180°F (about 5–6 minutes). Immediately remove from heat and strain the custard through a fine-mesh sieve into the inner bowl of the prepared ice bath.

5. Cool the custard in the ice bath until room temperature, stirring occasionally. Cover and chill in the refrigerator for at least 4 hours, or overnight.

6. Place storage container in the freezer to chill. Freeze the mixture in an ice cream maker according to the manufacturer's instructions until ice cream is thick and creamy and has increased in volume by about a third.

7. Enjoy immediately or freeze 2 hours in chilled storage container for a firmer scoop. For storage tips see p. 28.

2 cups (473 ml) heavy cream

1 cup (236 ml) whole milk

¾ cup (177 ml) pure dark maple syrup

¼ tsp fine sea salt

5 large egg yolks (90 g)

Matcha, a Japanese green tea powder, is touted for its bazillion antioxidants. We use culinary-grade matcha, which has a vibrant green colour from the high chlorophyll levels in the tea leaves and a somewhat bitter, vegetal taste. That bitterness can become too pronounced if it's cooked, so remove the base from the heat before adding the tea. If you want to live forever, pair a scoop of this with Golden Milk (p. 150)!

# MATCHA

VEGAN   MAKES ABOUT 1 QUART

1. Prepare an ice bath (p. 25).

2. Scoop out 1½ cups (350 g) coconut cream from the chilled cans of coconut milk and reserve coconut water for another use. Whisk together coconut cream, coconut milk, sugar and salt in a medium-sized saucepan. Stir over medium-high heat for 5–7 minutes, until sugar is dissolved and no visible bits of coconut cream remain. Remove from heat and strain through a fine-mesh sieve into the inner bowl of the prepared ice bath.

3. Sift matcha powder directly into the mixture, then whisk well. Stir in vanilla. Cool the ice cream base in the ice bath until room temperature, stirring occasionally. Cover and chill in the refrigerator for at least 4 hours, or overnight.

4. Once the base is chilled, you may notice a layer of solids on the top. Give it all a quick mix to incorporate before churning. Place storage container in the freezer to chill. Freeze the mixture in an ice cream maker according to the manufacturer's instructions until ice cream is thick and creamy and has increased in volume by about a third. The base is ready when (with the machine turned off) you can scoop a big spoon of it and watch the ice cream fall back into the bowl in thick trails.

5. Enjoy immediately or freeze 2 hours in chilled storage container for a firmer scoop. For storage tips see p. 28.

2 (400 ml) cans coconut milk, chilled for 24 hours

1 (400 ml) can coconut milk, room temperature

1½ cups (300 g) sugar

¼ tsp fine sea salt

2 Tbsp + 1 tsp (14 g) matcha green tea powder

½ tsp pure vanilla extract

If you love coconut—the aroma, the flavour, the texture—you'll love this recipe. Plus, your kitchen will smell amazing as the oils in the roasting coconut flakes perfume the air.

# TOASTED COCONUT

VEGAN   MAKES ABOUT 1 QUART

1. Toast shredded coconut in a large skillet over medium-low heat for 5 minutes, stirring often, until the flakes are golden brown and very fragrant. Cool completely.

   Cooled coconut can be stored in an airtight container at room temperature for 1 week.

2. Prepare an ice bath (p. 25).

3. Scoop out 1½ cups (350 g) coconut cream from the chilled cans of coconut milk and reserve coconut water for another use. Whisk together coconut cream, coconut milk, sugar and salt in a medium-sized saucepan. Stir for 5–7 minutes over medium-high heat, until sugar is dissolved and no visible bits of coconut cream remain. Remove from heat and strain through a fine-mesh sieve into the inner bowl of the prepared ice bath.

4. Cool the ice cream base in the ice bath until room temperature, stirring occasionally. Cover and chill in the refrigerator for at least 4 hours, or overnight.

5. Once the base is chilled, you may notice a layer of solids on the top. Give it all a quick mix to incorporate before churning. Place storage container in the freezer to chill. Freeze the mixture in an ice cream maker according to the manufacturer's instructions until ice cream is thick and creamy and has increased in volume by about a third. The base is ready when (with the machine turned off) you can scoop a big spoon of it and watch the ice cream fall back into the bowl in thick trails.

6. Once churned, add in toasted coconut and churn for a further 30 seconds until incorporated.

7. Enjoy immediately or freeze 2 hours in chilled storage container for a firmer scoop. For storage tips see p. 28.

¼ cup (21 g) shredded unsweetened coconut

2 (400 ml) cans coconut milk, chilled for 24 hours

1 (400 ml) can coconut milk, room temperature

1½ cups (300 g) sugar

¼ tsp fine sea salt

Malt and chocolate are best friends, and nothing says Easter quite like candy eggs. So this is our fun Easter ice cream—crushed mini eggs in a malted milk–chocolate base. For classic parlour-style malted milk, we recommend Ovaltine.

# MALTED MILK CHOCOLATE & MINI EGG

GLUTEN   MAKES ABOUT 1 QUART

1. Prepare an ice bath (p. 25).

2. In a medium-sized saucepan, whisk together cream, milk, sugar, malted milk powder and salt. Stir over medium-high heat for about 5 minutes, until steam begins to rise from the surface. Remove from heat. Add in chopped chocolate and set aside for 1 minute, or until chocolate chunks begin to melt. Whisk well to incorporate the melted chocolate.

3. While the dairy is warming, whisk the egg yolks in a medium-sized bowl. To temper the yolks, slowly pour 1 cup of the heated cream mixture into the yolks while whisking vigorously. Continue adding heated cream and whisking until about half of the hot cream has been added. Transfer the yolk mixture to the pan.

4. Cook the mixture over medium heat, stirring continuously with a heatproof spatula, until the mixture is thick enough to coat the spatula or a digital thermometer reads 180°F (about 5-6 minutes). Immediately remove from heat and strain the custard through a fine-mesh sieve into the inner bowl of the prepared ice bath.

5. Stir in vanilla. Cool the custard in the ice bath until room temperature, stirring occasionally. Cover and chill in the refrigerator for at least 4 hours, or overnight.

6. Place storage container in the freezer to chill. Freeze the mixture in an ice cream maker according to the manufacturer's instructions until ice cream is thick and creamy and has increased in volume by about a third.

7. Once churned, add in crushed mini eggs and churn for a further 30 seconds until incorporated.

8. Enjoy immediately or freeze 2 hours in chilled storage container for a firmer scoop. For storage tips see p. 28.

2 cups (473 ml) heavy cream

1 cup (236 ml) whole milk

½ cup (100 g) sugar

½ cup (62 g) malted milk powder

¼ tsp fine sea salt

¾ cup (140 g) finely chopped milk chocolate (30% cocoa)

5 large egg yolks (90 g)

1 tsp pure vanilla extract

1 cup (180 g) candy-coated mini chocolate eggs, crushed (see Tip)

### CANDY CRUSH

To crush mini eggs, lay them on a baking sheet or any flat surface with walls (to prevent runaways). Use a heavy-bottomed saucepan to press down on the eggs to crush.

Hibiscus flowers (aka Jamaican sorrel or roselle hibiscus), when dried, make for a brilliant cranberry-coloured tea. When in bloom, at Christmastime, they're brewed with ginger and rum for a favourite Caribbean punch.

This vegan ice cream celebrates the first warm days of spring. We pair the tart, citrusy flowers with sweet passion fruit—both pulp and seeds. Look for dried hibiscus flowers in shops specializing in Caribbean foods or in the Asian aisles of supermarkets.

# HIBISCUS & PASSION FRUIT

VEGAN   MAKES ABOUT 1 QUART

1. Prepare an ice bath (p. 25).

2. Scoop out 1½ cups (350 g) coconut cream from the chilled cans of coconut milk and reserve coconut water for another use. Whisk together coconut cream, coconut milk, sugar and salt in a medium-sized saucepan. Stir over medium-high heat for 5-7 minutes, until sugar is dissolved and no visible bits of coconut cream remain.

3. Meanwhile, cut passion fruits in half and scoop out the pulp and seeds. Add to the saucepan along with the hibiscus. Reduce heat to low and steep passion fruit and hibiscus for 20 minutes.

4. Remove from heat and strain through a fine-mesh sieve into the inner bowl of the prepared ice bath, pressing down on the passion fruit and hibiscus with a stiff rubber spatula to extract as much flavour as possible.

5. Cool the ice cream base in the ice bath until room temperature, stirring occasionally. Cover and chill in the refrigerator for at least 4 hours, or overnight.

6. Once the base is chilled, you may notice a layer of solids on the top. Give it all a quick mix to incorporate before churning. Place storage container in the freezer to chill. Freeze the mixture in an ice cream maker according to the manufacturer's instructions until ice cream is thick and creamy and has increased in volume by about a third. The base is ready when (with the machine turned off) you can scoop a big spoon of it and watch the ice cream fall back into the bowl in thick trails.

7. Enjoy immediately or freeze 2 hours in chilled storage container for a firmer scoop. For storage tips see p. 28.

2 (400 ml) cans coconut milk, chilled for 24 hours

1 (400 ml) can coconut milk, room temperature

1½ cups (300 g) sugar

¼ tsp fine sea salt

2 ripe passion fruits

1 cup (40 g) dried food-grade hibiscus flowers

The nostalgic flavour of cereal milk, the crunch of puffed rice and a swirl of gooey, sweet marshmallow. We haven't provided a recipe for rice crispy squares because the one on the side of the cereal box will do just fine. You can buy marshmallow fluff or use egg whites to make your own.

# SNAP, MERRY, POP

GLUTEN   MAKES ABOUT 1 QUART

**MARSHMALLOW FLUFF**

1. Whisk together egg whites, sugar, cream of tartar and salt.

2. Bring 3 inches of water to a simmer in a medium-sized saucepan and rest the bowl of egg white mixture over it. Whisk the mixture over the simmering water for 1–2 minutes, until frothy and sugar is dissolved. The sugar is fully dissolved when you can rub the egg whites between your fingers and not feel any grittiness. Remove the bowl from the pan and wipe the condensation off the bottom.

3. Using either a hand mixer or a stand mixer fitted with the whisk attachment, whisk egg white mixture on low speed for 1 minute. (Make sure the equipment is very clean and dry, otherwise the meringue won't aerate properly.) Increase speed to high and whisk for 5 minutes, or until egg whites are glossy and look like a loose whipped cream. Whisk in vanilla.

4. Transfer marshmallow fluff to a piping bag fitted with a ½-inch round tip. If you are preparing the marshmallow fluff ahead of time, store it in a sealed airtight container at room temperature for up to 2 days. Makes about 1 cup.

**SNAP, MERRY, POP ICE CREAM**

5. In a medium-sized saucepan, combine cream, milk, Rice Krispies, sugar and salt. Stir over medium heat for 5 minutes, or until steam begins to rise from the surface. Remove from heat. Cover and set aside for 30 minutes to steep cereal.

6. Prepare an ice bath (p. 25).

7. Reheat the dairy mixture over medium-high heat for 3–5 minutes, or until steam begins to rise from the surface.

**MARSHMALLOW FLUFF**

2 large egg whites (70 g)

6 Tbsp (75 g) sugar

½ tsp cream of tartar

¼ tsp fine sea salt

1 tsp pure vanilla extract

**SNAP, MERRY, POP ICE CREAM**

2 cups (473 ml) heavy cream

1 cup (236 ml) whole milk

1 cup (120 g) Rice Krispies cereal

½ cup (100 g) sugar

¼ tsp fine sea salt

5 large egg yolks (90 g)

1 tsp pure vanilla extract

1½ cups (45 g) Rice Krispies squares, cut into ¼-inch cubes

1 qty Marshmallow Fluff (see here)

8. While the dairy is warming, whisk the egg yolks in a medium-sized bowl. To temper the yolks, slowly pour 1 cup of the heated cream mixture into the yolks while whisking vigorously. Continue adding heated cream and whisking until about half of the hot cream has been added. Transfer the yolk mixture to the pan.

9. Cook the mixture over medium heat, stirring continuously with a heatproof spatula, until the mixture is thick enough to coat the spatula or a digital thermometer reads 180°F (about 5–6 minutes). Immediately remove from heat and strain the custard through a fine-mesh sieve into the inner bowl of the prepared ice bath, pressing down on the cereal with a stiff rubber spatula to extract as much flavour as possible.

10. Stir in vanilla. Cool the custard in the ice bath until room temperature, stirring occasionally. Cover and chill in the refrigerator for at least 4 hours, or overnight.

11. Place storage container in the freezer to chill. Freeze the ice cream in an ice cream maker according to the manufacturer's instructions until ice cream is thick and creamy and has increased in volume by about a third.

12. Once churned, add in cubed Rice Krispies squares and churn for a further 30 seconds until incorporated. Spoon a few scoops of just-churned ice cream into your storage container, then squeeze a few lines of marshmallow fluff over ice cream. Don't worry about swirling in fluff, you want pockets of it. Repeat layering the ice cream and marshmallow fluff.

13. Enjoy immediately or freeze 2 hours for a firmer scoop. For storage tips see p. 28.

A classic blend of raspberries and sweet cream cheese, its richness tempered with lemon. You could serve this dreamy ice cream with extra raspberry sauce (p. 196) or a spoonful of lemon curd (p. 197). Leave out the graham crumbs to keep it gluten-free.

# RASPBERRY CHEESECAKE

GLUTEN    MAKES ABOUT 1 QUART

### GRAHAM CRUMBLE

1. Combine all the ingredients in a small bowl. Transfer the crumbs to a dinner plate and press together to form a uniform crust. Freeze uncovered for 20 minutes, or until firm. Break into ½-inch pieces.

   Graham crumbs can be stored in an airtight container at room temperature for up to 1 week. Makes about ¾ cup.

### RASPBERRY CHEESECAKE ICE CREAM

2. Prepare an ice bath (p. 25).

3. In a medium-sized saucepan, combine cream, milk, sugar, cream cheese, lemon zest and salt. Using an immersion blender, blend until completely combined, with no visible chunks. (Or blend ingredients in a regular blender, then transfer mixture to a saucepan.) Cook over medium-high heat for 5 minutes, or until steam begins to rise from the surface. Remove from heat.

4. While the dairy is warming, whisk the egg yolks in a medium-sized bowl. To temper the yolks, slowly pour 1 cup of the heated cream mixture into the yolks while whisking vigorously. Continue adding heated cream and whisking until about half of the hot cream has been added. Transfer the yolk mixture to the pan.

5. Cook the mixture over medium heat, stirring continuously with a heatproof spatula, until the mixture is thick enough to coat the spatula or a digital thermometer reads 180°F (about 5–6 minutes). Immediately remove from heat and strain the custard through a fine-mesh sieve into the inner bowl of the prepared ice bath.

### GRAHAM CRUMBLE

½ cup (60 g) graham crumbs

2 ½ Tbsp (35 g) unsalted butter, melted

2 tsp sugar

⅛ tsp fine sea salt

### RASPBERRY CHEESECAKE ICE CREAM

2 cups (473 ml) heavy cream

1 cup (236 ml) whole milk

¾ cup (150 g) sugar

¾ cup (170 g) full-fat cream cheese

1 Tbsp lemon zest (about 1 lemon)

¼ tsp fine sea salt

5 large egg yolks (90 g)

½ tsp pure vanilla extract

1 qty Graham Crumble (see here)

1 qty Raspberry Sauce (p. 196)

6. Stir in vanilla. Cool the custard in the ice bath until room temperature, stirring occasionally. Cover and chill in the refrigerator for at least 4 hours, or overnight.

7. Place storage container in the freezer to chill. Freeze the mixture in an ice cream maker according to the manufacturer's instructions until ice cream is thick and creamy and has increased in volume by about a third.

8. Once churned, add in graham crumble and churn for a further 30 seconds until incorporated. Spoon a few scoops of just-churned ice cream into your storage container. Dollop some raspberry sauce on top. Using a butter knife, gently swirl sauce into ice cream. Repeat by layering with ice cream and more sauce.

9. Enjoy immediately or freeze 2 hours for a firmer scoop. For storage tips see p. 28.

Raspberry Cheesecake
(p. 48)

Nanaimo Bar
(p. 52)

This is our nod to Nanaimo, BC, and its famous namesake bars. Our coconut base is enriched with a vegan-friendly custard powder and studded with graham and coconut clusters enrobed in chocolate. A dark chocolate swirl is the finishing touch.

# NANAIMO BAR

<u>VEGAN / GLUTEN</u>   MAKES ABOUT 1 QUART

### GRAHAM AND COCONUT CLUSTERS

1. Line a baking sheet with parchment paper.

2. In a medium-sized bowl, crumble graham crackers into small pieces, ranging between ½ inch and 1 inch. Mix in shredded coconut.

3. In a small saucepan, melt chocolate and coconut oil over low heat, stirring frequently. Pour over graham crackers and coconut and toss to coat. Use a teaspoon to portion the clusters into little mounds and place on a baking sheet. Let the clusters completely harden in the refrigerator.

   Clusters can be stored in an airtight container at room temperature for up to 1 week. Makes about 1 cup.

### NANAIMO BAR ICE CREAM

4. Prepare an ice bath (p. 25).

5. In a medium-sized saucepan, whisk together custard powder and sugar. Scoop out 1½ cups (350 g) coconut cream from the chilled cans of coconut milk and reserve coconut water for another use. Add coconut cream, coconut milk and salt to saucepan and whisk continuously over medium-high heat for 5–7 minutes, until custard powder and sugar are dissolved and no visible bits of coconut cream remain. Remove from heat and strain through a fine-mesh sieve into the inner bowl of the prepared ice bath.

### GRAHAM AND COCONUT CLUSTERS

6 squares (45 g) honey-free graham crackers

¼ cup (21 g) shredded unsweetened coconut

⅓ cup (56 g) coarsely chopped dark chocolate (70–75% cocoa)

½ tsp coconut oil

### NANAIMO BAR ICE CREAM

½ cup + 2 Tbsp (75 g) vegan custard powder, such as Bird's

1½ cups (300 g) sugar

2 (400 ml) cans coconut milk, chilled for 24 hours

1 (400 ml) can coconut milk, room temperature

¼ tsp fine sea salt

2 tsp pure vanilla extract

1 qty Graham and Coconut Clusters (see here)

1 qty Chocolate Sauce (p. 198)

6. Stir in vanilla. Cool the ice cream base in the ice bath until room temperature, stirring occasionally. Cover and chill in the refrigerator for at least 4 hours, or overnight.

7. Once the base is chilled, you may notice a layer of solids on the top. Give it all a quick mix to incorporate before churning. Place storage container in the freezer to chill. Freeze the mixture in an ice cream maker according to the manufacturer's instructions until ice cream is thick and creamy and has increased in volume by about a third. The base is ready when (with the machine turned off) you can scoop a big spoon of it and watch the ice cream fall back into the bowl in thick trails.

8. Once churned, add in graham and coconut clusters and churn for a further 30 seconds until incorporated. Spoon a few scoops of just-churned ice cream into your storage container. Dollop chocolate sauce on top. Using a butter knife, gently swirl sauce into ice cream. Repeat by layering with ice cream and more sauce.

9. Enjoy immediately or freeze 2 hours for a firmer scoop. For storage tips see p. 28.

A recipe for those who licked the beaters as kids, and perhaps still do. You could, of course, make your favourite from-scratch cake recipe, but somehow the boxed mix and canned icing lend this ice cream a certain 1970s nostalgia.

# CAKE BATTER & CHOCOLATE FROSTING

GLUTEN   MAKES ABOUT 1 QUART

1.  Prepare an ice bath (p. 25).

2.  In a medium-sized saucepan, combine cream, milk, sugar and salt. Stir over medium-high heat for about 5 minutes, until steam begins to rise from the surface. Remove from heat.

3.  While the dairy is warming, whisk the egg yolks in a medium-sized bowl. To temper the yolks, slowly pour 1 cup of the heated cream mixture into the yolks while whisking vigorously. Continue adding heated cream and whisking until about half of the hot cream has been added. Transfer the yolk mixture to the pan.

4.  Cook the mixture over medium heat, stirring continuously with a heatproof spatula, until the mixture is thick enough to coat the spatula or a digital thermometer reads 180°F (about 5-6 minutes). Immediately remove from heat and strain the custard through a fine-mesh sieve into the inner bowl of the prepared ice bath.

5.  Sift cake mix directly over the ice cream base and whisk well. Stir in vanilla. Cool the custard in the ice bath until room temperature, stirring occasionally. Cover and chill in the refrigerator for at least 4 hours, or overnight.

6.  Place storage container in the freezer to chill. Freeze the mixture in an ice cream maker according to the manufacturer's instructions until ice cream is thick and creamy and has increased in volume by about a third.

7.  Once churned, add in sprinkles and churn for a further 30 seconds until incorporated. Spoon a few scoops of just-churned ice cream into your storage container. Dollop frosting on top with a spoon or from a piping bag fitted with a ½-inch round tip. Using a butter knife, gently swirl the frosting into the ice cream. Repeat by layering with ice cream and more frosting.

8.  Enjoy immediately or freeze 2 hours for a firmer scoop. For storage tips see p. 28.

2 cups (473 ml) heavy cream

1 cup (236 ml) whole milk

½ cup (100 g) sugar

¼ tsp fine sea salt

5 large egg yolks (90 g)

⅔ cup (95 g) boxed yellow cake mix, heat treated (see Tip)

1 Tbsp pure vanilla extract

¼ cup (42 g) rainbow sprinkles

½ cup (120 g) canned chocolate frosting

### HEAT-TREATING CAKE MIX

Preheat oven to 350°F. Scatter cake mix on a baking sheet, then bake for 5 minutes. Cool cake mix and set aside.

What a colour! This violet ice cream reminds our Merry Dairy team member Iona of her childhood in the Philippines, where ube—purple yam—is a staple in desserts. Look for fresh ube in Asian markets, or frozen ube in most supermarkets.

# UBE

VEGAN   MAKES ABOUT 1 QUART

## UBE JAM

1. In a heavy-bottomed saucepan, combine ube, coconut milk, sugar, maple syrup and salt. Bring to a boil over high heat, then reduce heat to medium-low. Simmer jam for 20 minutes, stirring occasionally, until it has thickened significantly. Remove from heat.

2. Using an immersion or regular blender, purée until smooth.

3. You can use the warm jam in the ice cream base immediately. If you're preparing the jam for later use, cool completely and store in a glass jar in the refrigerator for up to 2 weeks. Makes about 1 cup.

## UBE ICE CREAM

4. Prepare an ice bath (p. 25).

5. Scoop out 1½ cups (350 g) coconut cream from the chilled cans of coconut milk and reserve coconut water for another use. Whisk together all the ingredients in a medium-sized saucepan. Stir for 5-7 minutes over medium-high heat, until sugar is dissolved and no visible bits of coconut cream remain. Remove from heat and strain through a fine-mesh sieve into the inner bowl of the prepared ice bath.

6. Cool the ice cream base in the ice bath until room temperature, stirring occasionally. Cover and chill in the refrigerator for at least 4 hours, or overnight.

7. Once the base is chilled, you may notice a layer of solids on the top. Give it all a quick mix to incorporate before churning. Place storage container in the freezer to chill. Freeze the mixture in an ice cream maker according to the manufacturer's instructions until ice cream is thick and creamy and has increased in volume by about a third. The base is ready when (with the machine turned off) you can scoop a big spoon of it and watch the ice cream fall back into the bowl in thick trails.

8. Enjoy immediately or freeze 2 hours in chilled storage container for a firmer scoop. For storage tips see p. 28.

### UBE JAM

1 lb (454 g) fresh ube, grated, or frozen ube, puréed

1 (400 ml) can coconut milk, room temperature

1 cup (200 g) sugar

2 Tbsp (30 ml) pure maple syrup

¼ tsp fine sea salt

### UBE ICE CREAM

2 (400 ml) cans coconut milk, chilled for 24 hours

1 (400 ml) can coconut milk, room temperature

1½ cups (300 g) sugar

¾ cup (255 g) Ube Jam (see here)

¼ tsp fine sea salt

When pink and green shoots appear in winter-weary gardens, we know spring has arrived. And so has our annual Rhubarb Exchange: neighbours drop off rhubarb from their gardens; we give them a pint of this pleasure once it's churned. A delicious win-win!

Here, rhubarb roasted in honey and balsamic vinegar is added to the custard base. Beet juice pinks it up. For a sophisticated dessert, finish with extra rhubarb purée and mint leaves—and maybe a drizzle of chocolate sauce (p. 198).

# ROASTED RHUBARB

MAKES ABOUT 1 QUART

### BALSAMIC-ROASTED RHUBARB

1. Preheat oven to 400°F. Line a baking sheet with parchment paper.

2. Scatter rhubarb over the baking sheet and then drizzle with honey and balsamic vinegar. Roast for 15 minutes, or until rhubarb is softened and browned. You can use the warm rhubarb in the ice cream base immediately.

   If you're preparing the rhubarb for later use, cool completely and store in an airtight container in the refrigerator for up to 1 week. Makes about 6 tablespoons.

### ROASTED RHUBARB ICE CREAM

3. Prepare an ice bath (p. 25).

4. In a medium-sized saucepan, combine cream, milk and roasted rhubarb. Blend with an immersion blender until very smooth. (Or you can blend ingredients in a regular blender, then transfer to a saucepan.) Add sugar and salt. Stir the mixture over medium-high heat for 5 minutes, or until steam begins to rise from the surface. Remove from heat.

5. While the dairy is warming, whisk the egg yolks in a medium-sized bowl. To temper the yolks, slowly pour 1 cup of the heated cream mixture into the yolks while whisking vigorously. Continue adding heated cream and whisking until about half of the hot cream has been added. Transfer the yolk mixture to the pan.

### BALSAMIC-ROASTED RHUBARB

2 cups (200 g) chopped rhubarb, about 3 trimmed stocks

3 Tbsp (63 g) pure local honey

1 Tbsp balsamic vinegar

### ROASTED RHUBARB ICE CREAM

2 cups (473 ml) heavy cream

1 cup (236 ml) whole milk

1 qty Balsamic-Roasted Rhubarb (see here)

½ cup (100 g) sugar

¼ tsp fine sea salt

5 large egg yolks (90 g)

1 Tbsp beet juice, for colour (optional) (see Tip, p. 77)

Fresh mint leaves, for garnish (optional)

6.  Cook the mixture over medium heat, stirring continuously with a heatproof spatula, until the mixture is thick enough to coat the spatula or a digital thermometer reads 180°F (about 5–6 minutes). Immediately remove from heat and strain the custard through a fine-mesh sieve into the inner bowl of the prepared ice bath, pressing down on any rhubarb bits with a stiff rubber spatula to extract as much flavour as possible.

7.  Add a few teaspoons of beet juice (if using) for a light pink hue. Cool the custard in the ice bath until room temperature, stirring occasionally. Cover and chill in the refrigerator for at least 4 hours, or overnight.

8.  Place storage container in the freezer to chill. Freeze the mixture in an ice cream maker according to the manufacturer's instructions until ice cream is thick and creamy and has increased in volume by about a third.

9.  Garnish with mint (if using) and enjoy immediately, or freeze 2 hours in chilled storage container for a firmer scoop. For storage tips see p. 28.

**BALSAMIC-ROASTED RHUBARB SAUCE OR SWIRL**

If making balsamic-roasted rhubarb as a sauce or swirl, scrape the warm rhubarb and any caramelized bits into a bowl. Using an immersion blender, purée until mostly smooth. (Or blend it in a regular blender.) Set aside to cool.

Rhubarb can be stored in a sealed glass jar in the refrigerator for up to 1 week. Makes about 6 tablespoons.

Roasted Rhubarb
(p. 56)

Trash Panda
(p. 60)

Our Ottawa neighbourhood of Hintonburg is where the Gemini award–winning TV series *The Raccoons* originated. Here, our masked bandits are affectionately known (mostly by garbage collectors) as "trash pandas." We created this trashy-fun ice cream in their honour. It looks a little like the debris left after their weekly curbside garbage inspections. Into our creamy base go chocolate and raspberry sauces, homemade cookies and pretzels. This ice cream will restore your mood after cleaning up their mess.

# TRASH PANDA

GLUTEN   MAKES ABOUT 1 QUART

### CHOCOLATE-COVERED PRETZELS

1. Line a baking sheet with parchment paper.

2. In a small saucepan, melt chocolate and coconut oil over low heat, stirring frequently. Add pretzels and stir to coat. Spread pretzels on the baking sheet in a single layer. Set aside at room temperature for 30 minutes, or until chocolate has set (or chill in the refrigerator for 10 minutes). Break up the pretzel slab into ¼-inch pieces.

   Pretzels can be stored in an airtight container at room temperature for up to 3 days. Makes ½ cup.

### TRASH PANDA ICE CREAM

3. In a medium-sized saucepan, combine cream, milk, sugar, pretzel sticks and salt. Stir over medium-high heat for about 5 minutes, until steam begins to rise from the surface. Remove from heat. Cover and steep for 20 minutes.

4. Reheat the mixture over medium-high heat for 3–5 minutes, or until steam begins to rise from the surface.

5. Prepare an ice bath (p. 25).

6. While the dairy is warming, whisk the egg yolks in a medium-sized bowl. To temper the yolks, slowly pour 1 cup of the heated cream mixture into the yolks while whisking vigorously. Continue adding heated cream and whisking until about half of the hot cream has been added. Transfer the yolk mixture to the pan.

### CHOCOLATE-COVERED PRETZELS

¼ cup (42 g) finely chopped dark chocolate (70–75% cocoa)

½ tsp coconut oil

¼ cup (28 g) pretzel sticks or twists

### TRASH PANDA ICE CREAM

2 cups (473 ml) heavy cream

1 cup (236 ml) whole milk

½ cup (100 g) sugar

½ cup (20 g) pretzel sticks

¼ tsp fine sea salt

5 large egg yolks (90 g)

¼ cup (70 g) Chocolate-Covered Pretzels (see here)

½ cup (about 115 g) "chef's choice" cookies, crumbled into bite-sized pieces

1 qty Chocolate Sauce (p. 198)

1 qty Raspberry Sauce (p. 196)

7. Cook the mixture over medium heat, stirring continuously with a heatproof spatula, until the mixture is thick enough to coat the spatula or a digital thermometer reads 180°F (about 5–6 minutes). Immediately remove from heat and strain the custard through a fine-mesh sieve into the inner bowl of the prepared ice bath, pressing down on the pretzels with a stiff rubber spatula to extract as much flavour as possible.

8. Cool the custard in the ice bath until room temperature, stirring occasionally. Cover and chill in the refrigerator for at least 4 hours, or overnight.

9. Place storage container in the freezer to chill. Freeze the mixture in an ice cream maker according to the manufacturer's instructions until ice cream is thick and creamy and has increased in volume by about a third.

10. Once churned, add in chocolate-covered pretzels and cookies and churn for a further 30 seconds until incorporated. Spoon a few scoops of just-churned ice cream into your storage container. Dollop chocolate and raspberry sauces on top. Using a butter knife, add sauces and gently swirl into ice cream. Repeat by layering with ice cream and more sauce.

11. Enjoy immediately or freeze 2 hours for a firmer scoop. For storage tips see p. 28.

What can we say? It's a classic. There are so many things to love about this ice cream. It's worth noting that the edible cookie dough in this recipe is designed to be eaten raw. It will not bake up into a regular cookie!

# CHOCOLATE CHIP COOKIE DOUGH

GLUTEN (OPTIONAL) **MAKES ABOUT 1 QUART**

### EDIBLE COOKIE DOUGH

1. Line a baking sheet with parchment paper.

2. In a medium-sized bowl, combine butter, both sugars and salt. Use a wooden spoon or stiff rubber spatula to mix until well combined and paste-like.

3. Add in vanilla, cream and molasses. Stir in flour and chocolate chips. The dough will be thick and sticky.

4. To shape the dough, lay a medium-sized piece of parchment on your clean work surface and mound the dough on top. Lay another piece of parchment over the dough and use a rolling pin to flatten it to a ½-inch thickness. Do not worry about the shape of the cookie dough at this point; it will get cut up into uniform cubes later. Slide the parchment and cookie dough slab onto a baking sheet and refrigerate for 20 minutes.

5. Transfer the parchment and cookie dough to a cutting board, remove the top piece of parchment and cut the dough into ½-inch cubes. Transfer the cookie dough bits to an airtight container.

   Cookie dough bits can be stored in the freezer for up to 2 months. Makes about 2 cups.

### COOKIE DOUGH ICE CREAM

6. Prepare an ice bath (p. 25).

7. In a medium-sized saucepan, combine cream, milk, sugar, molasses and salt over medium-high heat for 5 minutes, or until steam begins to rise from the surface. Remove from heat.

### EDIBLE COOKIE DOUGH

¼ cup (57 g) unsalted butter, room temperature

¼ cup (50 g) sugar

¼ cup (50 g) firmly packed light brown sugar

⅛ tsp fine sea salt

1 Tbsp pure vanilla extract

1 Tbsp heavy cream

1 tsp fancy molasses

½ cup (60 g) all-purpose flour or gluten-free flour blend, heat treated (see Tip)

6 Tbsp (60 g) mini chocolate chips

### COOKIE DOUGH ICE CREAM

2 cups (473 ml) heavy cream

1 cup (236 ml) whole milk

¼ cup (50 g) sugar

2 Tbsp (30 ml) fancy molasses

¼ tsp fine sea salt

5 large egg yolks (90 g)

2 tsp pure vanilla extract

1 qty cubed Edible Cookie Dough (see here)

¼–½ cup (59–118 ml) Chocolate Sauce (p. 198)

8. While dairy is warming, whisk egg yolks in a medium heatproof bowl. To temper the yolks, slowly pour 1 cup of the heated cream mixture into the yolks while whisking vigorously. Continue adding heated cream and whisking until about half of the hot cream has been added. Transfer the yolk mixture to the pan.

9. Cook the mixture over medium heat, stirring continuously with a heatproof spatula, until the mixture is thick enough to coat the spatula or a digital thermometer reads 180°F (about 5-6 minutes). Immediately remove from heat and strain the custard through a fine-mesh sieve into the inner bowl of the prepared ice bath.

10. Stir in vanilla. Cool the custard in the ice bath until room temperature, stirring occasionally. Cover and chill in the refrigerator for at least 4 hours, or overnight.

11. Place storage container in the freezer to chill. Freeze the mixture in an ice cream maker according to the manufacturer's instructions until ice cream is thick and creamy and has increased in volume by about a third.

12. Once churned, add in cookie dough and churn for a further 30 seconds until incorporated. Spoon a few scoops of just-churned ice cream into your storage container. Dollop some chocolate sauce on top. Using a butter knife, gently swirl sauce into ice cream. Repeat by layering with ice cream and more sauce.

13. Enjoy immediately or freeze 2 hours for a firmer scoop. For storage tips see p. 28.

**HEAT-TREATING FLOUR**

Bet you always thought you shouldn't eat raw cookie dough because of the eggs. Turns out you can't eat raw flour either.

Flours are made from raw grains, and the milling process does not kill bacteria. To heat-treat flour, scatter it on a baking sheet, then bake for 5 minutes in a 350°F oven. Cool the flour, sift, then proceed with the recipe.

We created this flavour as an homage to our annual Italian Week in Ottawa. We make our own nut-free biscotti (p. 202) and drop the cookies into the ice cream—its flavour ramped up with zest and the Italian liqueur limoncello. The blackberry sauce is swirled in, creating dark violet ribbons in a pale yellow base. It's pretty stunning stuff.

# LIMONCELLO BLACKBERRY BISCOTTI

GLUTEN   MAKES ABOUT 1 QUART

1. Prepare an ice bath (p. 25).

2. In a medium-sized saucepan, combine cream, milk, sugar and salt. Stir over medium heat for 5 minutes, or until steam begins to rise from the surface. Remove from heat.

3. While the dairy is warming, whisk the egg yolks in a medium-sized bowl. To temper the yolks, slowly pour 1 cup of the heated cream mixture into the yolks while whisking vigorously. Continue adding heated cream and whisking until about half of the hot cream has been added. Transfer the yolk mixture to the pan.

4. Cook the mixture over medium heat, stirring continuously with a heatproof spatula, until the mixture is thick enough to coat the spatula or a digital thermometer reads 180°F (about 5–6 minutes). Immediately remove from heat and strain the custard through a fine-mesh sieve into the inner bowl of the prepared ice bath.

5. Cool the custard in the ice bath until room temperature. Stir in lemon zest and limoncello. Chill in the refrigerator for 4 hours, or overnight.

6. Place storage container in the freezer to chill. Freeze the mixture in an ice cream maker according to the manufacturer's instructions until ice cream is thick and creamy and has increased in volume by about a third.

7. Once churned, add in biscotti and churn for 30 seconds until incorporated. Spoon a few scoops of just-churned ice cream into your storage container. Dollop some blackberry sauce on top. Using a butter knife, gently swirl sauce into ice cream. Repeat by layering with ice cream and more sauce.

8. Enjoy immediately with biscotti and more sauce, or freeze 2 hours for a firmer scoop. For storage tips see p. 28.

2 cups (473 ml) heavy cream

1 cup (236 ml) whole milk

¼ cup (50 g) sugar

¼ tsp fine sea salt

5 large egg yolks (90 g)

1 Tbsp lemon zest (about 1 lemon)

¼ cup (59 ml) limoncello
(see Booze tip, p. 115)

1 (40-g) Lemon Biscotti (p. 202),
cut into bite-sized pieces

1 qty Blackberry Sauce (p. 196)

Marketed back when we were kids, toaster tarts were the great breakfast treat for the busy family on the go. We've made our own version of Canada's favourite toaster tart, and they're pretty irresistible. We toss one tart into the vanilla custard base, while the second one gets folded in at the end. (The third and fourth are snacks for the cook.) Add a swirl of your favourite berry sauce (p. 196) for extra pizzazz.

# FROSTED BERRY TART

GLUTEN   MAKES ABOUT 1 QUART

1.  Prepare an ice bath (p. 25).

2.  In a blender, combine half of the toaster tart pieces, along with the cream and milk. Blend for 1 minute, or until no visible chunks of toaster tarts remain. Transfer the mixture to a medium-sized saucepan, then add sugar and salt. Warm over medium-high heat for 5 minutes, or until steam begins to rise from the surface. Remove from heat.

3.  While the dairy is warming, whisk the egg yolks in a medium-sized bowl. To temper the yolks, slowly pour 1 cup of the heated cream mixture into the yolks while whisking vigorously. Continue adding heated cream and whisking until about half of the hot cream has been added. Transfer the yolk mixture to the pan.

4.  Cook the mixture over medium heat, stirring continuously with a heatproof spatula, until the mixture is thick enough to coat the spatula or a digital thermometer reads 180°F (about 5–6 minutes). Immediately remove from heat and strain the custard through a fine-mesh sieve into the inner bowl of the prepared ice bath, pressing down on the toaster tart pulp with a stiff rubber spatula to extract as much flavour as possible. Scrape the outside of the sieve to collect the thick custard and add it to the base.

5.  Stir in vanilla. Cool the custard in the ice bath until room temperature, stirring occasionally. Cover and chill in the refrigerator for at least 4 hours, or overnight.

6.  Place storage container in the freezer to chill. Freeze the mixture in an ice cream maker according to the manufacturer's instructions until ice cream is thick and creamy and has increased in volume by about a third.

7.  Once churned, add in the remaining toaster tart pieces and churn for a further 30 seconds until incorporated.

8.  Enjoy immediately or freeze 2 hours in chilled storage container for a firmer scoop. For storage tips see p. 28.

**2 Frosted Berry Toaster Tarts (p. 205), finely chopped, divided**

**2 cups (473 ml) heavy cream**

**1 cup (236 ml) whole milk**

**½ cup (100 g) sugar**

**¼ tsp fine sea salt**

**5 large egg yolks (90 g)**

**1 ½ tsp pure vanilla extract**

Few debates in Canada are more heated than those on the butter tart: Should it or should it not contain raisins? We at The Merry Dairy do *not* take sides, though we do present a butter tart ice cream that so happens to not have raisins. But there is no disagreement over the deliciousness of the gooey, sweet filling and flaky crust when tossed with the maple base. A cone of this ice cream is the perfect end to any spring barbecue.

# BUTTER TART

GLUTEN   MAKES ABOUT 1 QUART

1. Prepare an ice bath (p. 25).

2. In a medium-sized saucepan, combine cream, milk, maple syrup, brown sugar and salt. Stir over medium-high heat for about 5 minutes, until steam begins to rise from the surface. Remove from heat.

3. While the dairy is warming, whisk the egg yolks in a medium-sized bowl. To temper the yolks, slowly pour 1 cup of the heated cream mixture into the yolks while whisking vigorously. Continue adding heated cream and whisking until about half of the hot cream has been added. Transfer the yolk mixture to the pan.

4. Cook the mixture over medium heat, stirring continuously with a heatproof spatula, until the mixture is thick enough to coat the spatula or a digital thermometer reads 180°F (about 5–6 minutes). Immediately remove from heat and strain the custard through a fine-mesh sieve into the inner bowl of the prepared ice bath.

5. Stir in vanilla. Cool the custard in the ice bath until room temperature, stirring occasionally. Cover and chill in the refrigerator for at least 4 hours, or overnight.

6. Place storage container in the freezer to chill. Freeze the mixture in an ice cream maker according to the manufacturer's instructions until ice cream is thick and creamy and has increased in volume by about a third.

7. Once churned, add in butter tart pieces and churn for a further 30 seconds until incorporated.

8. Enjoy immediately or freeze 2 hours in chilled storage container for a firmer scoop. For storage tips see p. 28.

2 cups (473 ml) heavy cream

1 cup (236 ml) whole milk

¼ cup (59 ml) pure maple syrup

¼ cup (50 g) firmly packed light brown sugar

¼ tsp fine sea salt

5 large egg yolks (90 g)

1 tsp pure vanilla extract

2–3 Butter Tarts (p. 204), broken into bite-sized pieces

# SUMMER

Traditionally associated with Middle Eastern and Indian cuisine, preserved lemons (or salt-pickled lemons) add a big jolt of flavour to stews, tagines and curries. But they add lovely tart and salty notes to rich sweet treats too. Here, the preserved lemon and earthy thyme make for a sophisticated scoop.

# PRESERVED LEMON & THYME

**VEGAN**   **MAKES ABOUT 1 QUART**

1. Scoop out 1 ½ cups (350 g) coconut cream from the chilled cans of coconut milk and reserve coconut water for another use. Whisk together coconut cream, coconut milk, sugar, thyme and lemon liquid in a medium-sized saucepan. Stir over medium-high heat for 5-7 minutes, until sugar is dissolved and no visible bits of coconut cream remain. Turn the heat to low and steep thyme for 15 minutes. Remove from heat and strain through a fine-mesh sieve into the inner bowl of the prepared ice bath.

2. Prepare an ice bath (p. 25).

3. Mix in lemon rind. Cool the ice cream base in the ice bath until room temperature, stirring occasionally. Cover and chill in the refrigerator for at least 4 hours, or overnight.

4. Once the base is chilled, you may notice a layer of solids on the top. Give it all a quick mix to incorporate before churning. Place storage container in the freezer to chill. Freeze the mixture in an ice cream maker according to the manufacturer's instructions until ice cream is thick and creamy and has increased in volume by about a third. The base is ready when (with the machine turned off) you can scoop a big spoon of it and watch the ice cream fall back into the bowl in thick trails.

5. Enjoy immediately or freeze 2 hours in chilled storage container for a firmer scoop. For storage tips see p. 28.

2 (400 ml) cans coconut milk, chilled for 24 hours

1 (400 ml) can coconut milk, room temperature

1 ½ cups (300 g) sugar

5 sprigs thyme

2 tsp preserved-lemon liquid

3 Tbsp (35 g) finely chopped preserved-lemon rind

"How come your mint chocolate chip isn't green?" Yup, we hear that a lot. The answer is simple: ours contains no artificial colour. We use fresh mint leaves steeped in milk and cream—that's all, folks. No imitation peppermint extract and no green food colouring. If the lack of colour really troubles you, we suggest eating it with your eyes closed.

# FRESH MINT CHIP

MAKES ABOUT 1 QUART

1. In a medium-sized saucepan, combine cream, milk, sugar and salt. Stir over medium-high heat for about 5 minutes, until steam begins to rise from the surface. Remove from heat. Add in mint and submerge as much as possible. Cover and steep for 2 hours.

2. Pluck out any big pieces of mint and squeeze out as much mixture as you can. It is okay if little bits remain—they get strained out later. Reheat cream over medium-high heat for 5 minutes, or until steam begins to rise from the surface.

3. Prepare an ice bath (p. 25).

4. While the dairy is warming, whisk the egg yolks in a medium-sized bowl. To temper the yolks, slowly pour 1 cup of the heated cream mixture into the yolks while whisking vigorously. Continue adding heated cream and whisking until about half of the hot cream has been added. Transfer the yolk mixture to the pan.

5. Cook the mixture over medium heat, stirring continuously with a heatproof spatula, until the mixture is thick enough to coat the spatula or a digital thermometer reads 180°F (about 5–6 minutes). Immediately remove from heat and strain the custard through a fine-mesh sieve into the inner bowl of the prepared ice bath.

6. Cool the custard in the ice bath until room temperature, stirring occasionally. Cover and chill in the refrigerator for at least 4 hours, or overnight.

7. Place storage container in the freezer to chill. Freeze the mixture in an ice cream maker according to the manufacturer's instructions until ice cream is thick and creamy and has increased in volume by about a third.

8. Once churned, add in chocolate chips and churn for a further 30 seconds until incorporated.

9. Enjoy immediately or freeze 2 hours in chilled storage container for a firmer scoop. For storage tips see p. 28.

2 cups (473 ml) heavy cream

1 cup (236 ml) whole milk

½ cup (100 g) sugar

¼ tsp fine sea salt

Bunch of mint (85 g)

5 large egg yolks (90 g)

½ cup (90 g) mini chocolate chips

### COOL MINT

There are over 600 varieties of mint! Spearmint is the gold standard for ice cream, but experiment with chocolate mint, lemon mint, peppermint and any other varieties you can find.

Our inspiration for this ice cream came from Amelia's mother's honeybees. They had been feeding on the lavender in her garden, and the fragrance of their honey was fantastic.

Experiment with seasonal honeys if you want to switch up the flavour. However, we don't suggest experimenting with the lavender infusion time. Lavender can be pretty strong stuff, and if left too long, your ice cream could end up tasting like a bath bomb.

# HONEY LAVENDER

MAKES ABOUT 1 QUART

1. Prepare an ice bath (p. 25).

2. In a medium-sized saucepan, combine cream, milk, honey, lavender and salt. Stir over medium-high heat for about 5 minutes, until steam begins to rise from the surface. Remove from heat.

3. While the dairy is warming, whisk the egg yolks in a medium-sized bowl. To temper the yolks, slowly pour 1 cup of the heated cream mixture into the yolks while whisking vigorously. Continue adding heated cream and whisking until about half of the hot cream has been added. Transfer the yolk mixture to the pan.

4. Cook the mixture over medium heat, stirring continuously with a heatproof spatula, until the mixture is thick enough to coat the spatula or a digital thermometer reads 180°F (about 5–6 minutes). Immediately remove from heat and strain the custard through a fine-mesh sieve into the inner bowl of the prepared ice bath.

5. Cool the custard in the ice bath until room temperature, stirring occasionally. Cover and chill in the refrigerator for at least 4 hours, or overnight.

6. Place storage container in the freezer to chill. Freeze the mixture in an ice cream maker according to the manufacturer's instructions until ice cream is thick and creamy and has increased in volume by about a third.

7. Enjoy immediately or freeze 2 hours in chilled storage container for a firmer scoop. For storage tips see p. 28.

2 cups (473 ml) heavy cream

1 cup (236 ml) whole milk

½ cup (118 ml) pure local honey

2 Tbsp (8 g) dried food-grade lavender buds (see Tip)

¼ tsp fine sea salt

5 large egg yolks (90 g)

### HOW TO DRY LAVENDER

Lavender buds are most flavourful right before they open. Trim the flowers at the base of the stem, just above the leaves. Use twine to tie up small bundles of flowers and hang upside down in a dark, dry and warm spot for 7–10 days. The dried buds can then be easily plucked off the stems.

It's true that it's mostly adults who opt for our plant-based ice creams. But we have more and more kids warming up to vegan treats…and why deny them the pleasure of a kid-pleasing cone? So we came up with this somewhat outrageous flavour. When the cotton candy is added at the end of the churning process, it dissolves into the ice cream in pockets of flossy fun.

# CREAM SODA & COTTON CANDY

VEGAN    MAKES ABOUT 1 QUART

1. Prepare an ice bath (p. 25).

2. Scoop out 1½ cups (350 g) coconut cream from the chilled cans of coconut milk and reserve coconut water for another use. Whisk cream soda, coconut cream, sugar and salt in a medium-sized saucepan. Stir for 5–7 minutes over medium-high heat, until sugar is dissolved and no visible bits of coconut cream remain. Remove from heat and strain through a fine-mesh sieve into the inner bowl of the prepared ice bath.

3. Cool the ice cream base in the ice bath until room temperature, stirring occasionally. Cover and chill in the refrigerator for at least 4 hours, or overnight.

4. Once the base is chilled, you may notice a layer of solids on the top. Give it all a quick mix to incorporate before churning. Place storage container in the freezer to chill. Freeze the mixture in an ice cream maker according to the manufacturer's instructions until ice cream is thick and creamy and has increased in volume by about a third. The base is ready when (with the machine turned off) you can scoop a big spoon of it and watch the ice cream fall back into the bowl in thick trails.

5. Once churned, add in cotton candy and churn for a further 30 seconds until incorporated.

6. Enjoy immediately or freeze 2 hours in chilled storage container for a firmer scoop. For storage tips see p. 28.

2 (400 ml) cans coconut milk, chilled for 24 hours

1½ cups (355 ml can) cream soda

1¼ cups (250 g) sugar

¼ tsp fine sea salt

1 cup (12 g) torn cotton candy

## HOW SUGAR AFFECTS THE FREEZING POINT

When blended with sugar, water has a lower freezing point than it does on its own, which means that sugar has the ability to make ice cream soft. The more sugar in your ice cream, the lower the freezing point and the softer the finished product. If you reduce the sugar too much, though, the ice cream will be too hard to scoop and could even resemble one big ice cube. If you do reduce the sugar, add 1 or 2 tablespoons of alcohol to make sure the result is scoopable.

We replace the coconut milk with lemonade from concentrate in this blushing-pink ice cream. It may seem odd to be massaging the lemon zest with the sugar, but the jagged edges of the sugar crystals aggravate the zest, teasing out more of its oils. More oils mean more flavour. You'll notice we don't call for the base to be strained. You want to see and taste that zest!

# PINK LEMONADE

VEGAN   MAKES ABOUT 1 QUART

1. Prepare an ice bath (p. 25).

2. Put sugar and lemon zest in a medium-sized bowl. Using your fingers, massage sugar into lemon zest until no clumps of zest remain.

3. Scoop out 1½ cups (350 g) coconut cream from the chilled cans of coconut milk and set aside. Reserve coconut water for another use.

4. Put frozen pink lemonade concentrate in a medium-sized sauce-pan and melt over medium heat. Add the sugar mixture, coconut cream and salt. Stir over medium-high heat for 5-7 minutes, until sugar is dissolved and no visible bits of coconut cream remain. Remove from heat and pour into the inner bowl of the prepared ice bath.

5. Cool the ice cream base in the ice bath until room temperature, stirring occasionally. Cover and chill in the refrigerator for at least 4 hours, or overnight.

6. Once the base is chilled, you may notice a layer of solids on the top. Give it all a quick mix to incorporate before churning. Place storage container in the freezer to chill. Freeze the mixture in an ice cream maker according to the manufacturer's instructions until ice cream is thick and creamy and has increased in volume by about a third. The base is ready when (with the machine turned off) you can scoop a big spoon of it and watch the ice cream fall back into the bowl in thick trails.

7. Garnish with mint and lemon slice (if using) and enjoy immediately, or freeze 2 hours in chilled storage container for a firmer scoop. For storage tips see p. 28.

1 ¼ cups (250 g) sugar

2 Tbsp (12 g) tightly packed lemon zest (about 2 large lemons)

2 (400 ml) cans coconut milk, chilled for 24 hours

1 (295 ml) can frozen pink lemonade concentrate

¼ tsp fine sea salt

Fresh mint leaves and lemon slices, for garnish (optional)

"Pink ice cream," as little Ruthie calls it, is the favourite of one of our favourite visitors. The rest of us call this lovely summery ice cream "Strawberry Ripple." It's made with July's ripest berries and threaded with a rosy ribbon of strawberry swirl. You can also add beet juice to seriously pink up things.

# STRAWBERRY RIPPLE

MAKES ABOUT 1 QUART

1. Combine strawberries, lemon juice and sugar in a medium-sized saucepan. Set aside for 20 minutes, or until the strawberries have released their juices.

2. Prepare an ice bath (p. 25).

3. Add cream, milk and salt to the strawberries. Using an immersion blender, purée until smooth. (Or you can blend ingredients in a regular blender, then transfer to the saucepan.)

4. Stir over medium-high heat for about 5 minutes, until steam begins to rise from the surface. Remove from heat.

5. While the dairy is warming, whisk the egg yolks in a medium-sized bowl. To temper the yolks, slowly pour 1 cup of the heated cream mixture into the yolks while whisking vigorously. Continue adding heated cream and whisking until about half of the hot cream has been added. Transfer the yolk mixture to the pan.

6. Cook the mixture over medium heat, stirring continuously with a heatproof spatula, until the mixture is thick enough to coat the spatula or a digital thermometer reads 180°F (about 5–6 minutes). Immediately remove from heat and strain the custard through a fine-mesh sieve into the inner bowl of the prepared ice bath.

7. Cool the custard in the ice bath until room temperature, stirring occasionally. Cover and chill in the refrigerator for at least 4 hours, or overnight.

8. Place storage container in the freezer to chill. Freeze the mixture in an ice cream maker according to the manufacturer's instructions until ice cream is thick and creamy and has increased in volume by about a third.

9. Spoon a few scoops of just-churned ice cream into your storage container. Dollop strawberry sauce on top. Using a butter knife, gently swirl sauce into ice cream. Repeat by layering with ice cream and more sauce.

10. Enjoy immediately or freeze 2 hours for a firmer scoop. For storage tips see p. 28.

15-20 (453 g) strawberries, green tops removed and coarsely chopped

1 Tbsp fresh lemon juice (about ½ a lemon)

1 cup (200 g) sugar

2 cups (473 ml) heavy cream

1 cup (236 ml) whole milk

¼ tsp fine sea salt

5 large egg yolks (90 g)

1 qty Strawberry Sauce (p. 196)

### PINK IT UP

To punch up the pinkness of your ice cream, dye the base with beet juice. Grate a large beet (wearing gloves if you don't care for dyed hands) over a plate lined with a few sheets of paper towel. Gather up the edges of the paper towel so that the grated beets are enclosed. Squeeze the beets directly over the strained ice cream base before chilling (step 7) until you have your desired colour. Beet juice is so vibrant that just a little juice goes a long way.

One of our founding flavours developed by Margaret, one of our founding churners! We encourage you to use local wild blueberries. Their season is fleeting, but their flavour is superior to that of cultivated blueberries. If using frozen wild blueberries, you may need to increase the cooking time by a few minutes.

# WILD BLUEBERRY LEMON

MAKES ABOUT 1½ QUARTS

### WILD BLUEBERRY LEMON SAUCE

1. In a medium-sized saucepan, combine blueberries, sugar and lemon juice. Bring to a boil over medium heat. Reduce heat to low and simmer for 10 minutes, stirring occasionally, until sauce is syrupy.

2. Using an immersion blender, purée until smooth. (Or you can blend ingredients in a regular blender. Remove the filler cap and cover with a tea towel to avoid a mess when blending.)

   Sauce can be stored in a sealed glass jar at room temperature for up to 2 weeks. Makes about 2 cups.

### WILD BLUEBERRY LEMON ICE CREAM

3. Prepare an ice bath (p. 25).

4. In a medium-sized saucepan, combine cream, milk, sugar, wild blueberry lemon sauce and salt. Stir over medium-high heat for about 5 minutes, until steam begins to rise from the surface. Remove from heat.

5. While the dairy is warming, whisk the egg yolks in a medium-sized bowl. To temper the yolks, slowly pour 1 cup of the heated cream mixture into the yolks while whisking vigorously. Continue adding heated cream and whisking until about half of the hot cream has been added. Transfer the yolk mixture to the pan.

**WILD BLUEBERRY LEMON SAUCE**

2 cups (332 g) fresh wild blueberries

½ cup (100 g) sugar

2 Tbsp (30 ml) fresh lemon juice (about 1 lemon)

**WILD BLUEBERRY LEMON ICE CREAM**

2 cups (473 ml) heavy cream

1 cup (236 ml) whole milk

½ cup (100 g) sugar

2 cups (473 ml) Wild Blueberry Lemon Sauce (see here)

¼ tsp fine sea salt

5 large egg yolks (90 g)

2 Tbsp (12 g) lemon zest (about 2 lemons)

6. Cook the mixture over medium heat, stirring continuously with a heatproof spatula, until the mixture is thick enough to coat the spatula or a digital thermometer reads 180°F (about 5–6 minutes). Immediately remove from heat and strain the custard through a fine-mesh sieve into the inner bowl of the prepared ice bath.

7. Stir in lemon zest. Cool the custard in the ice bath until room temperature, stirring occasionally. Cover and chill in the refrigerator for at least 4 hours, or overnight.

8. Place storage container in the freezer to chill. Freeze the mixture in an ice cream maker according to the manufacturer's instructions until ice cream is thick and creamy and has increased in volume by about a third. Fill the ice cream machine only two-thirds full. Ice cream can easily be frozen in batches. If you have a surplus of ice cream base, keep it in the refrigerator for up to 3 days and freeze the rest at a later date.

9. Enjoy immediately or freeze 2 hours in chilled storage container for a firmer scoop. For storage tips see p. 28.

Wild Blueberry Lemon
(p. 78)

Plum Crumble
(p. 82)

Plums are so rarely in the spotlight, typically playing second fiddle to peaches and pears. But they make a gorgeous ice cream, here paired with an oat crumble in a sort of deconstructed plum crisp. Use any remaining compote as a warm finishing sauce. Then add another scoop of ice cream and another sprinkling of crumble. And maybe one last dollop of sauce.

# PLUM CRUMBLE

GLUTEN (OPTIONAL)   MAKES ABOUT 1 QUART

### OAT CRUMBLE

1. Preheat oven to 350°F. Line a baking sheet with parchment paper.

2. Using either a hand mixer or a stand mixer fitted with the paddle attachment, mix oats, flour, brown sugar and salt on low speed until combined.

3. Drop butter into the oat mixture. Mix on medium-low speed for 4–5 minutes, until mixture forms pea-sized crumbles. Scatter crumble over prepared baking sheet. Bake for 7–8 minutes, until crumble is golden brown. Set aside to cool completely, then use your fingers to break up crumble into small chunks.

   Crumble can be stored in an airtight container at room temperature for up to 1 week. Makes about 1 cup.

### PLUM CRUMBLE ICE CREAM

4. Prepare an ice bath (p. 25).

5. In a medium-sized saucepan, combine cream, milk, sugar and salt. Stir over medium-high heat for about 5 minutes, until steam begins to rise from the surface. Remove from heat.

6. While the dairy is warming, whisk the egg yolks in a medium-sized bowl. To temper the yolks, slowly pour 1 cup of the heated cream mixture into the yolks while whisking vigorously. Continue adding heated cream and whisking until about half of the hot cream has been added. Transfer the yolk mixture to the pan.

### OAT CRUMBLE

½ cup (45 g) rolled oats

2 Tbsp (15 g) all-purpose flour or gluten-free flour

2 Tbsp (25 g) light brown sugar

⅛ tsp fine sea salt

3 Tbsp (42 g) cold unsalted butter, cut into ½-inch cubes

### PLUM CRUMBLE ICE CREAM

2 cups (473 ml) heavy cream

1 cup (236 ml) whole milk

½ cup (100 g) sugar

¼ tsp fine sea salt

5 large egg yolks (90 g)

½ cup (50 g) Oat Crumble (see here)

½ cup (118 ml) Plum Compote (p. 197)

7.  Cook the mixture for 5-6 minutes over medium heat, stirring continuously with a heatproof spatula, until the mixture is thick enough to coat the spatula, or a digital thermometer reads 180°F. Immediately remove from heat and strain the custard through a fine-mesh sieve into the inner bowl of the prepared ice bath.

8.  Cool the custard in the ice bath until room temperature, stirring occasionally. Cover and chill in the refrigerator for at least 4 hours, or overnight.

9.  Place storage container in the freezer to chill. Freeze the mixture in an ice cream maker according to the manufacturer's instructions until ice cream is thick and creamy and has increased in volume by about a third.

10. Once churned, add in oat crumble chunks and churn for a further 30 seconds until incorporated. Spoon a few scoops of just-churned ice cream into your storage container. Dollop some plum compote on top. Using a butter knife, gently swirl the compote into the ice cream. Repeat by layering with ice cream and more compote. Any remaining compote can be warmed up and used as a sauce on top of a scoop. Garnish with leftover crumble.

11. Enjoy immediately or freeze 2 hours for a firmer scoop. For storage tips see p. 28.

A kid favourite, always. We don't skimp on the cookies—every bite has to have one. We use our homemade Salted Oatmeal Chocolate Chip Cookies (p. 201) and Ginger Molasses Cookies (p. 200). In spring and fall, we even toss in Girl Guide cookies. As the cookies freeze in the custard, they take on moisture and turn into hunks of yummy cake.

# MILK & COOKIES

GLUTEN    MAKES ABOUT 1 QUART

1. Prepare an ice bath (p. 25).

2. In a medium-sized saucepan, combine cream, milk, sugar and salt. Stir over medium-high heat for about 5 minutes, until steam begins to rise from the surface. Remove from heat.

3. While the dairy is warming, whisk the egg yolks in a medium-sized bowl. To temper the yolks, slowly pour 1 cup of the heated cream mixture into the yolks while whisking vigorously. Continue adding heated cream and whisking until about half of the hot cream has been added. Transfer the yolk mixture to the pan.

4. Cook the mixture over medium heat, stirring continuously with a heatproof spatula, until the mixture is thick enough to coat the spatula or a digital thermometer reads 180°F (about 5-6 minutes). Immediately remove from heat and strain the custard through a fine-mesh sieve into the inner bowl of the prepared ice bath.

5. Stir in vanilla. Cool the custard in the ice bath until room temperature, stirring occasionally. Cover and chill in the refrigerator for at least 4 hours, or overnight.

6. Place storage container in the freezer to chill. Freeze the mixture in an ice cream maker according to the manufacturer's instructions until ice cream is thick and creamy and has increased in volume by about a third.

7. Once churned, add in crumbled cookies and churn for a further 30 seconds until incorporated.

8. Enjoy immediately or freeze 2 hours in chilled storage container for a firmer scoop. For storage tips see p. 28.

2 cups (473 ml) heavy cream

1 cup (236 ml) whole milk

½ cup (100 g) sugar

¼ tsp fine sea salt

5 large egg yolks (90 g)

2 tsp pure vanilla extract

½ cup (about 115 g) "chef's choice" cookies, crumbled into bite-sized pieces

The Merry Dairy gives all credit to team member Holly for this flavour. She adores her Strawberry Banana—its sweetness, its lovely dreamy creaminess. Be sure to use ripe bananas: as you would for banana bread, you do for ice cream. Topped with a ripe strawberry sauce, this is a decadent dessert. Or try it for breakfast!

# STRAWBERRY BANANA

VEGAN   MAKES ABOUT 1 QUART

1. Prepare an ice bath (p. 25).

2. Scoop out 1½ cups (350 g) coconut cream from the chilled cans of coconut milk and reserve coconut water for another use. Whisk together coconut cream, coconut milk, sugar and salt in a medium-sized saucepan. Add bananas and, using an immersion blender, purée until smooth. (Or you can blend ingredients in a regular blender, then transfer to the saucepan.) Stir over medium-high heat for 5–7 minutes, until sugar is dissolved and no visible bits of coconut cream remain. Remove from heat and strain through a fine-mesh sieve into the inner bowl of the prepared ice bath.

3. Cool the ice cream base in the ice bath until room temperature, stirring occasionally. Cover and chill in the refrigerator for at least 4 hours, or overnight.

4. Once the base is chilled, you may notice a layer of solids on the top. Give it all a quick mix to incorporate before churning. Place storage container in the freezer to chill. Freeze the mixture in an ice cream maker according to the manufacturer's instructions until ice cream is thick and creamy and has increased in volume by about a third. The base is ready when (with the machine turned off) you can scoop a big spoon of it and watch the ice cream fall back into the bowl in thick trails.

5. Spoon a few scoops of just-churned ice cream into your storage container. Dollop some strawberry sauce on top. Using a butter knife, gently swirl sauce into ice cream. Repeat by layering with ice cream and more sauce.

6. Enjoy immediately or freeze 2 hours for a firmer scoop. For storage tips see p. 28.

2 (400 ml) cans coconut milk, chilled for 24 hours

1 (400 ml) can coconut milk, room temperature

1½ cups (300 g) sugar

¼ tsp fine sea salt

3 ripe bananas

1 qty Strawberry Sauce (p. 196)

When peaches land in the markets, we all go bananas and The Merry Dairy kitchen has a giant peach party. It's peach iced tea, peach pops, peach sauce, peach pie... and of course, peach ice cream. We don't peel our peaches: the skins add flavour and colour. This ice cream classic is Ontario summer, frozen in time.

# ONTARIO PEACH

MAKES ABOUT 1 QUART

### MACERATED PEACHES

1. Place peaches in a food processor. Pulse until finely chopped, scraping down the sides of the bowl as needed.

2. In a small bowl, combine peaches, sugar and lemon juice. Cover the bowl and set aside for 30 minutes at room temperature, stirring occasionally. Strain the mixture through a fine-mesh sieve, pressing down on the peaches with a stiff rubber spatula to extract as much juice as possible. Set juice aside for ice cream base.

3. Transfer remaining peach solids to a container and refrigerate until you are ready to make the ice cream.

   Peach solids and juices can be stored separately in airtight containers in the refrigerator for up to 1 week.

### PEACH ICE CREAM

4. Prepare an ice bath (p. 25).

5. In a medium-sized saucepan, combine cream, milk, peach juice, sugar and salt. Stir over medium-high heat for about 5 minutes, until steam begins to rise from the surface. Remove from heat.

6. While the dairy is warming, whisk the egg yolks in a medium-sized bowl. To temper the yolks, slowly pour 1 cup of the heated cream mixture into the yolks while whisking vigorously. Continue adding heated cream and whisking until about half of the hot cream has been added. Transfer the yolk mixture to the pan.

### MACERATED PEACHES

2 ripe peaches, unpeeled, pitted and coarsely chopped

½ cup (100 g) sugar

2 Tbsp (30 ml) fresh lemon juice (about 1 lemon)

### PEACH ICE CREAM

2 cups (473 ml) heavy cream

1 cup (236 ml) whole milk

½ cup (118 ml) reserved peach juice from Macerated Peaches (see here)

½ cup (100 g) sugar

¼ tsp fine sea salt

5 large egg yolks (90 g)

½ cup (100 g) Macerated Peaches (see here)

7. Cook the mixture over medium heat, stirring continuously with a heatproof spatula, until the mixture is thick enough to coat the spatula or a digital thermometer reads 180°F (about 5-6 minutes). Immediately remove from heat and strain the custard through a fine-mesh sieve into the inner bowl of the prepared ice bath.

8. Cool the custard in the ice bath until room temperature, stirring occasionally. Cover and chill in the refrigerator for at least 4 hours, or overnight.

9. Place storage container in the freezer to chill. Freeze the mixture in an ice cream maker according to the manufacturer's instructions until ice cream is thick and creamy and has increased in volume by about a third.

10. Once churned, add in macerated peaches and churn for a further 30 seconds until incorporated.

11. Enjoy immediately or freeze 2 hours in chilled storage container for a firmer scoop. For storage tips see p. 28.

### MACERATION

"Maceration" is a fancy term for the mixing of sugar and fruit—it adds flavour, draws out excess liquid from the fruit and creates a delicious syrup. Maceration can also refer to the soaking of fruit in a liquid (such as vinegar, juice, liqueur), but in the case of fruit ice cream, we want the sugar to bond with the excess water that the fruit brings to the recipe. Too much water equals too much ice!

### AVOIDING THE DREADED FRUIT ICE CUBE

If untreated, the water in fruit will freeze solid in ice cream, creating an unpleasant fruit ice cube. Combining fruit with sugar or cooking the moisture off are two ways to ensure the fruit remains edible, even when matched against the coldest of freezers.

Ontario Peach
(p. 86)

S'mores
(p. 90)

The quintessential Canadian summer treat. Sitting around the campfire, roasting marshmallows, telling ghost stories, eating s'mores … it doesn't get much better. Unless you add ice cream to the mix! We use a kitchen torch (easily available and not too expensive) to toast the marshmallows, though you could use your oven's broiler—or the campfire.

# S'MORES

GLUTEN    MAKES ABOUT 1 QUART

### CHARRED MARSHMALLOWS

1.  Lay marshmallows in a single layer on a baking sheet (without parchment or a silicone baking mat). Use a kitchen torch to toast the marshmallows to your liking. Shimmy the pan to rotate the marshmallows and repeat until most of the white bits are charred or toasted. (Alternatively, char under the broiler; see Tip.) Set aside to cool.

    Marshmallows can be stored in an airtight container at room temperature for up to 1 week. Makes about ½ cup.

### CHOCOLATE-COVERED GRAHAM CRACKERS

2.  Arrange graham crackers on a plate and pour melted chocolate on top. Using an offset spatula or spoon, spread chocolate to fully coat the tops of the crackers. Chill in the refrigerator until the chocolate is set. Using your hands, break the crackers into approximately ¼-inch pieces.

    Crackers can be stored in an airtight container at room temperature for up to 1 week. Makes about ¼ cup.

### S'MORES ICE CREAM

3.  Prepare an ice bath (p. 25).

4.  In a medium-sized saucepan, combine cream, milk, sugar and salt. Stir over medium-high heat for about 5 minutes, until steam begins to rise from the surface. Remove from heat.

### CHARRED MARSHMALLOWS

½ cup (25 g) mini marshmallows

### CHOCOLATE-COVERED GRAHAM CRACKERS

6 squares (45 g) graham crackers

½ cup (90 g) coarsely chopped dark chocolate (70-75% cocoa), melted

### S'MORES ICE CREAM

2 cups (473 ml) heavy cream

1 cup (236 ml) whole milk

½ cup (100 g) sugar

¼ tsp fine sea salt

5 large egg yolks (90 g)

2 tsp pure vanilla extract

1 qty Charred Marshmallows (see here)

1 qty Chocolate-Covered Graham Crackers (see here)

5.  While the dairy is warming, whisk the egg yolks in a medium-sized bowl. To temper the yolks, slowly pour 1 cup of the heated cream mixture into the yolks while whisking vigorously. Continue adding heated cream and whisking until about half of the hot cream has been added. Transfer the yolk mixture to the pan.

6.  Cook the mixture over medium heat, stirring continuously with a heatproof spatula, until the mixture is thick enough to coat the spatula or a digital thermometer reads 180°F (about 5–6 minutes). Immediately remove from heat and strain the custard through a fine-mesh sieve into the inner bowl of the prepared ice bath.

7.  Stir in vanilla. Cool the custard in the ice bath until room temperature, stirring occasionally. Cover and chill in the refrigerator for at least 4 hours, or overnight.

8.  Place storage container in the freezer to chill. Freeze the mixture in an ice cream maker according to the manufacturer's instructions until ice cream is thick and creamy and has increased in volume by about a third.

9.  Once churned, add in charred marshmallows and chocolate-covered graham crackers and churn for a further 30 seconds until incorporated.

10. Enjoy immediately or freeze 2 hours in chilled storage container for a firmer scoop. For storage tips see p. 28.

**HOW TO OVEN-CHAR MARSHMALLOWS**

Preheat oven to broil. Lay marshmallows in a single layer on a baking sheet. Broil for 1–2 minutes, until slightly charred. (Broilers work quickly, so be sure to keep an eye on the marshmallows. Slightly burnt on the outside and gooey on the inside is ideal.) Remove the tray and give it a shimmy to rotate. Toast the other side for another 1–2 minutes.

This ice cream was inspired by a diner in rural South Carolina we stopped at during a road trip through the southern States. The place seemed frozen in some bygone era where everyone knew everyone else and the house special (sweet iced tea and warm peach pie) was a "help yourself" affair. The pitcher of minted tea was passed around from table to table. This recipe honours that sweet place.

# SOUTHERN SWEET TEA

<u>VEGAN</u>   MAKES ABOUT 1 QUART

### PEACH SAUCE

1.  In a medium-sized saucepan, stir all the ingredients together. Bring to a boil over medium heat and, stirring occasionally, cook for 3-4 minutes or until juices have thickened and peaches are glossy. Using an immersion blender, purée until smooth. (Or you can blend ingredients in a regular blender. Remove the filler cap and cover with a tea towel to avoid a mess when blending.)

2.  Set aside to cool completely.

    Sauce can be stored in a sealed glass jar in the refrigerator for up to 10 days. Makes about ½ cup.

### SOUTHERN SWEET TEA ICE CREAM

3.  Scoop out 1½ cups (350 g) coconut cream from the chilled cans of coconut milk and reserve coconut water for another use. Whisk together coconut cream, coconut milk, sugar and salt in a medium-sized pan. Stir over medium-high heat for 5-7 minutes, until sugar is dissolved and no visible bits of coconut cream remain. Reduce heat to low and add in tea leaves and mint. Steep for 15 minutes.

4.  While mixture is steeping, prepare an ice bath (p. 25).

**PEACH SAUCE**

1 ripe peach, unpeeled, pitted and finely chopped

2 Tbsp (30 ml) water

3 Tbsp (37 g) sugar

½ tsp cornstarch

⅛ tsp fine sea salt

**SOUTHERN SWEET TEA ICE CREAM**

2 (400 ml) cans coconut milk, chilled for 24 hours

1 (400 ml) can coconut milk, room temperature

1½ cups (300 g) sugar

½ tsp fine sea salt

¼ cup (24 g) black tea leaves

3 mint leaves

½ cup (118 ml) Peach Sauce (see here)

5. After 15 minutes of steeping, remove from heat and strain through a fine-mesh sieve into the inner bowl of the prepared ice bath, pressing down on the tea and mint with a stiff rubber spatula to extract as much flavour as possible.

6. Cool the ice cream base in the ice bath until room temperature, stirring occasionally. Cover and chill in the refrigerator for at least 4 hours, or overnight.

7. Once the base is chilled, you may notice a layer of solids on the top. Give it all a quick mix to incorporate before churning. Place storage container in the freezer to chill. Freeze the mixture in an ice cream maker according to the manufacturer's instructions until ice cream is thick and creamy and has increased in volume by about a third. The base is ready when (with the machine turned off) you can scoop a big spoon of it and watch the ice cream fall back into the bowl in thick trails.

8. Spoon a few scoops of just-churned ice cream into your storage container. Dollop some peach sauce on top. Using a butter knife, gently swirl sauce into ice cream. Repeat by layering with ice cream and more sauce.

9. Enjoy immediately or freeze 2 hours for a firmer scoop. For storage tips see p. 28.

**TURN UP THE TEA**

For a stronger tea flavour, add 2 teaspoons of tea leaves to the ice cream base after straining it. The leaves will continue to steep in the hot base and during the chill time, intensifying the flavour. Strain the base before churning.

In Ontario, corn season begins in late August. It's a mixed blessing, signalling that summer is fully ripe and also nearly over. In this recipe, we use both the corn kernels and their milky cobs, to wring out as much of that sweet corn flavour as possible. Use the freshest corn you can find.

This pale yellow, subtly sweet ice cream is lovely on a blueberry crumble or a peach pie, or melting on a wedge of warm cornbread.

# SWEET CORN & BLUEBERRY

MAKES ABOUT 1 QUART

1. Stand a cob vertically in a large kitchen bowl with the shank side down. Saw off the kernels with a chef's knife. The bowl will collect all the kernels and you will be left with the bare cob. Break cob in half. Repeat with the remaining cobs.

2. Place corn kernels and naked cobs into a medium-sized saucepan. Add cream, milk, sugar and salt. Stir over medium-high heat for about 5 minutes, until steam begins to rise from the surface. Remove from heat. Cover and steep for 1 hour.

3. Pluck out and discard cobs. Using an immersion blender, purée corn kernels and cream until smooth. (Or you can blend ingredients in a regular blender. Remove the filler cap and cover with a tea towel to avoid a mess when blending.)

4. Prepare an ice bath (p. 25).

5. Reheat the dairy mixture over medium-high heat for 3–5 minutes, or until steam begins to rise from the surface.

6. While the dairy is warming, whisk the egg yolks in a medium-sized bowl. To temper the yolks, slowly pour 1 cup of the heated cream mixture into the yolks while whisking vigorously. Continue adding heated cream and whisking until about half of the hot cream has been added. Transfer the yolk mixture to the pan.

3 cobs of sweet corn

2 cups (473 ml) heavy cream

1 cup (236 ml) whole milk

½ cup (100 g) sugar

¼ tsp fine sea salt

5 large egg yolks (90 g)

½ cup Wild Blueberry Lemon Sauce (p. 78)

7.  Cook the mixture over medium heat, stirring continuously with a heatproof spatula, until the mixture is thick enough to coat the spatula or a digital thermometer reads 180°F (about 5–6 minutes). Immediately remove from heat and strain the custard through a fine-mesh sieve into the inner bowl of the prepared ice bath, pressing down on the corn solids with a stiff rubber spatula to expel as much cream as possible.

8.  Cool the custard in the ice bath until room temperature, stirring occasionally. Cover and chill in the refrigerator for at least 4 hours, or overnight.

9.  Place storage container in the freezer to chill. Freeze the mixture in an ice cream maker according to the manufacturer's instructions until ice cream is thick and creamy and has increased in volume by about a third.

10. Spoon a few scoops of just-churned ice cream into your storage container. Dollop blueberry sauce on top. Using a butter knife, gently swirl sauce into ice cream. Repeat by layering with ice cream and more sauce.

11. Enjoy immediately or freeze 2 hours for a firmer scoop. For storage tips see p. 28.

You would not believe how many people have asked us over the years if we would make Tiger Tail ice cream. Love it or hate it, there's no denying its nostalgic appeal. Our challenge was to keep it natural, without artificial flavours or colours. We believe we've tamed this tiger, using natural anise extract, annatto, activated charcoal and real oranges.

# TIGER TAIL

MAKES ABOUT 1 QUART

### BLACK LICORICE RIBBON

1. Place measured butter and cream next to the stove. Keep an oven mitt (to protect your mixing hand from hot steam) and whisk nearby.

2. In a medium-sized saucepan, gently mix water and sugar over medium-high heat. Bring to a boil and watch carefully. Boil for 4-5 minutes, until sugar is dissolved and takes on a light golden colour. Remove from heat and carefully add butter. The mixture will billow up, then settle down. Put on the oven mitt and whisk well.

3. Whisk in cream and continue whisking until butter is melted and cream is combined. Mix in anise extract and activated charcoal. If the ribbon is not completely smooth, cook on medium heat until sugar clumps are dissolved. Set aside to cool.

   Licorice ribbon can be stored in a sealed glass jar at room temperature for up to 1 week or in the refrigerator for up to 2 weeks. Makes about ½ cup.

### TIGER TAIL ICE CREAM

4. Prepare an ice bath (p. 25).

5. In a medium-sized saucepan, combine cream, milk, orange juice, sugar and salt. Stir over medium-high heat for about 5 minutes, until steam begins to rise from the surface. Remove from heat.

6. While the dairy is warming, whisk the egg yolks in a medium-sized bowl. To temper the yolks, slowly pour 1 cup of the heated cream mixture into the yolks while whisking vigorously. Continue adding heated cream and whisking until about half of the hot cream has been added. Transfer the yolk mixture to the pan.

### BLACK LICORICE RIBBON

¼ cup (57 g) unsalted butter, room temperature

2 Tbsp (30 ml) heavy cream

1 Tbsp water

6 Tbsp (75 g) sugar

2 tsp anise extract

½ tsp activated coconut charcoal

### TIGER TAIL ICE CREAM

2 cups (473 ml) heavy cream

½ cup (118 ml) whole milk

½ cup (118 ml) fresh orange juice

¾ cup (150 g) sugar

¼ tsp fine sea salt

5 large egg yolks (90 g)

3 Tbsp (12 g) orange zest (about 1 large orange)

½-¾ tsp annatto powder

1 qty Black Licorice Ribbon (see here)

7. Cook the mixture over medium heat, stirring continuously with a heatproof spatula, until the mixture is thick enough to coat the spatula or a digital thermometer reads 180°F (about 5–6 minutes). Immediately remove from heat and strain the custard through a fine-mesh sieve into the inner bowl of the prepared ice bath.

8. Stir in orange zest and annatto and mix until it turns bright orange. Cool the custard in the ice bath until room temperature, stirring occasionally. Cover and chill in the refrigerator for at least 4 hours, or overnight.

9. Place storage container in the freezer to chill. Freeze the mixture in an ice cream maker according to the manufacturer's instructions until ice cream is thick and creamy and has increased in volume by about a third.

10. Spoon a few scoops of just-churned ice cream into your storage container. Dollop some licorice ribbon on top. Using a butter knife, gently swirl ribbon into ice cream. Repeat by layering with ice cream and more licorice ribbon.

11. Enjoy immediately or freeze 2 hours for a firmer scoop. For storage tips see p. 28.

Tiger Tail
(p. 96)

Honeycomb
(p. 100)

This ice cream is absolutely delicious. To start, honey makes ice cream incredibly smooth and creamy. To interrupt the smooth, we add sponge toffee—such fun to make! As the candy dissolves, it adds pockets of a toffee-like syrup, along with lovely crunchy bits that get stuck in the teeth in lingering ways.

# HONEYCOMB

MAKES ABOUT 1 QUART

**SPONGE TOFFEE**

1. Line a 9- × 5-inch loaf pan with parchment paper, leaving a generous overhang.

2. In a medium-sized saucepan, combine sugar, corn syrup and water and mix until the sugar is hydrated. Attach a candy thermometer to the pan. Make sure the tip of the thermometer is fully submerged but does not touch the bottom of the pan, to ensure an accurate reading. Place measured baking soda next to the stove. Keep an oven mitt (to protect your mixing hand from hot steam) and whisk nearby.

3. Bring syrup to a boil over high heat. Boil, resisting the urge to stir, for about 4 minutes, or until a candy thermometer reads 300°F and the sugar has started to caramelize, turning a golden colour. Gently swirl the pot if some spots are browning faster than others.

4. When the sugar is at temperature, put on the oven mitt and whisk in baking soda. The candy will erupt into a spongy hot web. Working swiftly, pour candy into the prepared pan. (It will harden quickly.) Do not spread out candy or shake the pan—you want to keep in as much air as possible. While still warm, sprinkle flaky salt on top, then set aside to cool completely.

5. Remove sponge toffee from the pan using the parchment overhang. Using your hands or a blunt kitchen utensil (like the handle of a whisk), break toffee into chunks no larger than a quarter. The candy will shatter into many different sizes—and you will want it all! Using both the candy dust and the larger pieces will give the ice cream a nice textural component.

   Sponge toffee can be stored in an airtight container at room temperature for up to 2 weeks. Makes about 1½ cups.

**SPONGE TOFFEE**

1 cup (200 g) sugar

¼ cup (59 ml) light corn syrup

3 Tbsp (45 ml) water

2¼ tsp baking soda (break up any obvious clumps)

Flaky sea salt, for garnish

**HONEYCOMB ICE CREAM**

6. Prepare an ice bath (p. 25).

7. In a medium-sized saucepan, combine cream, milk, honey and salt. Stir over medium-high heat for about 5 minutes, until steam begins to rise from the surface. Remove from heat.

8. While the dairy is warming, whisk the egg yolks in a medium-sized bowl. To temper the yolks, slowly pour 1 cup of the heated cream mixture into the yolks while whisking vigorously. Continue adding heated cream and whisking until about half of the hot cream has been added. Transfer the yolk mixture to the pan.

9. Cook the mixture over medium heat, stirring continuously with a heatproof spatula, until the mixture is thick enough to coat the spatula or a digital thermometer reads 180°F (about 5–6 minutes). Immediately remove from heat and strain the custard through a fine-mesh sieve into the inner bowl of the prepared ice bath.

10. Cool the custard in the ice bath until room temperature, stirring occasionally. Cover and chill in the refrigerator for at least 4 hours, or overnight.

11. Place storage container in the freezer to chill. Freeze the mixture in an ice cream maker according to the manufacturer's instructions until ice cream is thick and creamy and has increased in volume by about a third.

12. Once churned, add in sponge toffee and churn for a further 30 seconds until incorporated.

13. Enjoy immediately or freeze 2 hours in chilled storage container for a firmer scoop. For storage tips see p. 28.

**HONEYCOMB ICE CREAM**

2 cups (473 ml) heavy cream

1 cup (236 ml) whole milk

½ cup (118 ml) pure local honey

¼ tsp fine sea salt

5 large egg yolks (90 g)

¾ cup (60 g) Sponge Toffee (see here)

Credit for this recipe goes to Brooklyn's Van Leeuwen Ice Cream, its cookbook a treasured resource in our kitchen. After preparing a gifted bushel of sour cherries from Hidden Harvest, a group of volunteer pickers who harvest fruits and nuts that would otherwise go to waste, we spent the day making cherry compote—and the week with purple fingers. The floral fragrance and peppery zing of the Sichuan peppercorns work beautifully with the cherries. Scoop this ice cream onto cherry pie.

# SOUR CHERRY SICHUAN

MAKES ABOUT 1 QUART

### SOUR CHERRY COMPOTE

1. Combine cherries, sugar, orange zest and salt in a medium-sized saucepan. Bring to a simmer over medium-high heat, then reduce heat to medium and simmer for 10–15 minutes, until cherries have somewhat broken down and sauce is syrupy. Set aside to cool completely.

   Compote can be stored in a sealed glass jar in the refrigerator for up to 1 week. Makes about 1 cup.

### SOUR CHERRY SICHUAN ICE CREAM

2. Combine cream, milk, sugar, peppercorns and salt in a medium-sized saucepan. Stir over medium-high heat for about 5 minutes, until steam begins to rise from the surface. Remove from heat. Cover the saucepan and steep peppercorns for 15 minutes.

3. Reheat the mixture over medium-high heat for 3–5 minutes, or until steam begins to rise from the surface.

4. Prepare an ice bath (p. 25).

5. While the dairy is warming, whisk the egg yolks in a medium-sized bowl. To temper the yolks, slowly pour 1 cup of the heated cream mixture into the yolks while whisking vigorously. Continue adding heated cream and whisking until about half of the hot cream has been added. Transfer the yolk mixture to the pan.

### SOUR CHERRY COMPOTE

2 cups (350 g) fresh sour cherries, stemmed, pitted and coarsely chopped

1 cup (200 g) sugar

½ tsp orange zest

⅛ tsp fine sea salt

### SOUR CHERRY SICHUAN ICE CREAM

2 cups (473 ml) heavy cream

1 cup (236 ml) whole milk

½ cup (100 g) sugar

2 Tbsp (9 g) whole Sichuan peppercorns

¼ tsp fine sea salt

5 large egg yolks (90 g)

1 qty Sour Cherry Compote (see here)

6. Cook the mixture over medium heat, stirring continuously with a heatproof spatula, until the mixture is thick enough to coat the spatula or a digital thermometer reads 180°F (about 5-6 minutes). Immediately remove from heat and strain the custard through a fine-mesh sieve into the inner bowl of the prepared ice bath.

7. Cool the custard in the ice bath until room temperature, stirring occasionally. Cover and chill in the refrigerator for at least 4 hours, or overnight.

8. Place storage container in the freezer to chill. Freeze the mixture in an ice cream maker according to the manufacturer's instructions until ice cream is thick and creamy and has increased in volume by about a third.

9. Spoon a few scoops of just-churned ice cream into your storage container. Dollop some sour cherry compote on top. Using a butter knife, gently swirl the compote into the ice cream. Repeat by layering with ice cream and more sauce.

10. Enjoy immediately or freeze 2 hours for a firmer scoop. For storage tips see p. 28.

Sweet ripened pear and Moscato (a sweet, slightly fizzy Italian wine made with the fragrant Muscat grape) just go so well together. Here, pears are poached in the wine, then added to the ice cream base with a splash of the poaching liquid. Any leftover liquid, now infused with the pears, can be diluted with water for a delicious drink.

# MOSCATO-POACHED PEAR

MAKES ABOUT 1 QUART

### MOSCATO-POACHED PEAR PURÉE

1. In a medium-sized saucepan, combine pears, wine, sugar, honey and cinnamon stick. Scrape seeds from the split vanilla bean into the saucepan (see Tip, p. 23), then add the scraped pod.

2. Poach pears over medium heat for 45–50 minutes, until pears are softened and translucent and poaching liquid is syrupy. Remove and reserve vanilla pod.

3. Use tongs to pluck out pears and transfer them to a blender with ¼ cup (59 ml) of poaching liquid. Remove the filler cap so steam can escape and cover loosely with a tea towel. Blend until smooth. You can use the warm purée in the ice cream base immediately.

   If you're preparing the purée for later use, cool completely and store in a sealed glass jar in the refrigerator for up to 1 week. Makes about ½ cup.

### MOSCATO-POACHED PEAR ICE CREAM

4. Prepare an ice bath (p. 25).

5. In a medium-sized saucepan, combine cream, milk, pear purée, sugar and salt. Stir over medium-high heat for about 5 minutes, until steam begins to rise from the surface. Remove from heat.

6. While the dairy is warming, whisk the egg yolks in a medium-sized bowl. To temper the yolks, slowly pour 1 cup of the heated cream mixture into the yolks while whisking vigorously. Continue adding heated cream and whisking until about half of the hot cream has been added. Transfer the yolk mixture to the pan.

### MOSCATO-POACHED PEAR PURÉE

2 Bartlett pears, peeled, cored and quartered

2 cups (473 ml) Moscato white wine

¾ cup (150 g) sugar

¼ cup (59 ml) pure local honey

1 cinnamon stick

1 (4-inch) vanilla bean, cut lengthwise

### MOSCATO-POACHED PEAR ICE CREAM

2 cups (473 ml) heavy cream

1 cup (236 ml) whole milk

1 qty Moscato-Poached Pear Purée (see here)

½ cup (100 g) sugar

¼ tsp fine sea salt

5 large egg yolks (90 g)

¼ cup (59 ml) Moscato white wine

7. Cook the mixture over medium heat, stirring continuously with a heatproof spatula, until the mixture is thick enough to coat the spatula or a digital thermometer reads 180°F (about 5–6 minutes). Immediately remove from heat and strain the custard through a fine-mesh sieve into the inner bowl of the prepared ice bath, pressing down on the pear pulp with a stiff rubber spatula to extract as much flavour as possible.

8. Stir in wine. Add the vanilla pod back into the mixture to intensify the vanilla flavour. Cool the custard in the ice bath until room temperature, stirring occasionally. Cover and chill in the refrigerator for at least 4 hours, or overnight.

9. Remove vanilla pod (see Tip on p. 23 for reusing it). Place storage container in the freezer to chill. Freeze the mixture in an ice cream maker according to the manufacturer's instructions until ice cream is thick and creamy and has increased in volume by about a third.

10. Enjoy immediately or freeze 2 hours in chilled storage container for a firmer scoop. For storage tips see p. 28.

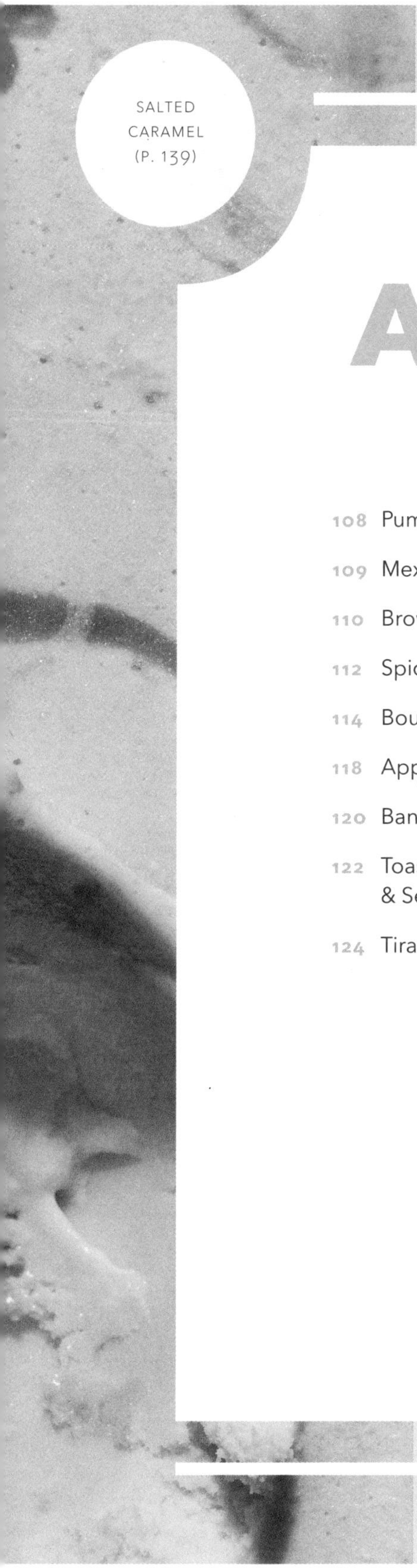

SALTED
CARAMEL
(P. 139)

# AUTUMN

For all you PSL lovers out there, we offer up this delicious autumn flavour. Using fresh spices makes all the difference, but you could absolutely use canned pumpkin purée (we like E.D. Smith).

# PUMPKIN SPICE

MAKES ABOUT 1 QUART

1. Prepare an ice bath (p. 25).

2. In a medium-sized saucepan, combine cream, milk, sugar, pumpkin purée, cinnamon, ginger, nutmeg and salt. Stir over medium-high heat for about 5 minutes, until steam begins to rise from the surface. Remove from heat.

3. While the dairy is warming, whisk the egg yolks in a medium-sized bowl. To temper the yolks, slowly pour 1 cup of the heated cream mixture into the yolks while whisking vigorously. Continue adding heated cream and whisking until about half of the hot cream has been added. Transfer the yolk mixture to the pan.

4. Cook the mixture over medium heat, stirring continuously with a heatproof spatula, until the mixture is thick enough to coat the spatula or a digital thermometer reads 180°F (about 5–6 minutes). Immediately remove from heat and strain the custard through a fine-mesh sieve into the inner bowl of the prepared ice bath.

5. Cool the custard in the ice bath until room temperature, stirring occasionally. Cover and chill in the refrigerator for at least 4 hours, or overnight.

6. Place storage container in the freezer to chill. Freeze the mixture in an ice cream maker according to the manufacturer's instructions until ice cream is thick and creamy and has increased in volume by about a third.

7. Enjoy immediately or freeze 2 hours in chilled storage container for a firmer scoop. For storage tips see p. 28.

1½ cups (354 ml) heavy cream

1 cup (236 ml) whole milk

½ cup (100 g) sugar

½ cup (112 g) pumpkin purée

2 tsp ground cinnamon

1 tsp ground ginger

¼ tsp ground nutmeg

¼ tsp fine sea salt

5 large egg yolks (90 g)

If you're anywhere near La Catrina Churros + Café Bar in Ottawa's ByWard Market, pick up a bag of their just-fried churros to pair with this spicy-warm vegan ice cream. Otherwise, it's pretty terrific with a swirl of Coconut Dulce de Leche (p. 132).

# MEXICAN DARK CHOCOLATE

VEGAN   MAKES ABOUT 1 QUART

1. Prepare an ice bath (p. 25).

2. Scoop out 1 ½ cups (350 g) coconut cream from the chilled cans of coconut milk and reserve coconut water for another use. Whisk together coconut cream, coconut milk, sugar, chili powder, cinnamon, cayenne pepper and salt in a medium-sized saucepan. Stir for 5-7 minutes, until sugar is dissolved and no visible bits of coconut cream remain. Remove from heat.

3. Add chocolate and set aside for 1 minute, or until chocolate chunks are significantly softened. Whisk to combine. Add vanilla. Strain through a fine-mesh sieve into the inner bowl of the prepared ice bath.

4. Cool the ice cream base in the ice bath until room temperature, stirring occasionally. Cover and chill in the refrigerator for at least 4 hours, or overnight.

5. Once the base is chilled, you may notice a layer of solids on the top. Give it all a quick mix to incorporate before churning. Place storage container in the freezer to chill. Freeze the mixture in an ice cream maker according to the manufacturer's instructions until ice cream is thick and creamy and has increased in volume by about a third. The base is ready when (with the machine turned off) you can scoop a big spoon of it and watch the ice cream fall back into the bowl in thick trails.

6. Enjoy immediately or freeze 2 hours in chilled storage container for a firmer scoop. For storage tips see p. 28.

2 (400 ml) cans coconut milk, chilled for 24 hours

1 (400 ml) can coconut milk, room temperature

1 ½ cups (300 g) sugar

2 ½ tsp chili powder

2 tsp ground cinnamon

¼ tsp ground cayenne pepper

¼ tsp fine sea salt

½ cup (85 g) finely chopped dark chocolate (70-75% cocoa)

½ tsp pure vanilla extract

Here's your recipe for making an ale float! A scoop of this bittersweet, butterscotchy ice cream floating in a stein of beer is pretty fantastic. Use a sweet stout, maybe even a chocolate stout if your local craft brewery makes one; stay clear of heavily hopped beers. Serve this ice cream with Brown-Butter Brownies (p. 203) for the ultimate pleasure.

# BROWN ALE & MOLASSES

GLUTEN  MAKES ABOUT 1 QUART

1. Bring ale to a boil in a medium-sized saucepan over medium heat. Boil for 20 minutes, or until ale has reduced by about three-quarters and looks syrupy.

2. Prepare an ice bath (p. 25).

3. Add cream, milk, brown sugar, molasses and salt to saucepan. Stir over medium-high heat for about 5 minutes, until steam begins to rise from the surface. Remove from heat.

4. While the dairy is warming, whisk the egg yolks in a medium-sized bowl. To temper the yolks, slowly pour 1 cup of the heated cream mixture into the yolks while whisking vigorously. Continue adding heated cream and whisking until about half of the hot cream has been added. Transfer the yolk mixture to the pan.

5. Cook the mixture over medium heat, stirring continuously with a heatproof spatula, until the mixture is thick enough to coat the spatula or a digital thermometer reads 180°F (about 5–6 minutes). Immediately remove from heat and strain the custard through a fine-mesh sieve into the inner bowl of the prepared ice bath.

6. Cool the custard in the ice bath until room temperature, stirring occasionally. Cover and chill in the refrigerator for at least 4 hours, or overnight.

7. Place storage container in the freezer to chill. Freeze the mixture in an ice cream maker according to the manufacturer's instructions until ice cream is thick and creamy and has increased in volume by about a third.

8. Enjoy immediately or freeze 2 hours in chilled storage container for a firmer scoop. For storage tips see p. 28.

1 cup (236 ml) brown ale

2 cups (473 ml) heavy cream

1 cup (236 ml) whole milk

¼ cup (50 g) firmly packed light brown sugar

¼ cup (59 ml) fancy molasses

¼ tsp fine sea salt

5 large egg yolks (90 g)

Roasted in a coat of cayenne, cinnamon, sugar and chili powder, these pepitas (pumpkin seeds from certain green varieties of squash) are excellent to nibble on while you prepare the base. So you might want to double the pepitas part of the recipe! Try a scoop of this autumn pleasure on a slice of apple cake.

# SPICED PEPITA

VEGAN   MAKES ABOUT 1 QUART

### SPICED PEPITAS

1. Preheat oven to 350°F. Line a baking sheet with parchment paper.

2. In a bowl, coat pepitas with coconut oil. Add remaining ingredients and mix well.

3. Spread mixture on the prepared baking sheet and bake for 10–12 minutes, shimmying the pan halfway through, until seeds are golden. Keep a close eye on them—they can burn very quickly.

   Baked pepitas can be stored in an airtight container at room temperature for up to 2 weeks. Makes about ½ cup.

### SPICED PEPITA ICE CREAM

4. Prepare an ice bath (p. 25).

5. Scoop out 1½ cups (350 g) coconut cream from the chilled cans of coconut milk and reserve coconut water for another use. Whisk together coconut cream, coconut milk, brown sugar, pumpkin purée, cinnamon, ginger, nutmeg and salt in a medium-sized saucepan. Stir for 5–7 minutes over medium-high heat, until sugar is dissolved and no visible bits of coconut cream remain. Remove from heat and strain through a fine-mesh sieve into the inner bowl of the prepared ice bath.

6. Cool the ice cream base in the ice bath until room temperature, stirring occasionally. Cover and chill in the refrigerator for at least 4 hours, or overnight.

### SPICED PEPITAS

½ cup (50 g) unsalted pepitas

1 tsp coconut oil, melted

1 tsp sugar

¼–½ tsp ground cayenne pepper

¼ tsp chili powder

¼ tsp ground cinnamon

¼ tsp salt

### SPICED PEPITA ICE CREAM

2 (400 ml) cans coconut milk, chilled for 24 hours

1 (400 ml) can coconut milk, room temperature

1½ cups (300 g) firmly packed light brown sugar

½ cup (112 g) canned pumpkin purée

4 tsp (10 g) ground cinnamon

1 tsp ground ginger

¼ tsp ground nutmeg

¼ tsp fine sea salt

1 qty Spiced Pepitas (see here)

7. Once the base is chilled, you may notice a layer of solids on the top. Give it all a quick mix to incorporate before churning. Place storage container in the freezer to chill. Freeze the mixture in an ice cream maker according to the manufacturer's instructions until ice cream is thick and creamy and has increased in volume by about a third. The base is ready when (with the machine turned off) you can scoop a big spoon of it and watch the ice cream fall back into the bowl in thick trails.

8. Once churned, add in spiced pepitas and churn for 30 seconds until incorporated.

9. Enjoy immediately or freeze 2 hours in chilled storage container for a firmer scoop. For storage tips see p. 28.

Tart, sweet, fruity… nothing says the good life quite like a bowlful of cherries. Particularly when those cherries are then cooked down until chunky and syrupy, the fruit almost candied, and added to a bourboned base. Serve this with a cherry on top? Maybe dipped in chocolate for the royal treatment.

# BOURBON BLACK CHERRY

MAKES ABOUT 1 QUART

### BOURBON CHERRIES

1. Combine cherries, brown sugar and water in a medium-sized saucepan. Boil over medium heat for 16–18 minutes, stirring frequently. Cook until syrupy and cherries have broken down slightly (some large chunks are okay). Remove from heat and stir in bourbon. If you're preparing for later use, cool completely and store in a sealed glass jar in the refrigerator for up to 5 days.

   Makes about 1½ cups.

### BOURBON CHERRY ICE CREAM

2. Prepare an ice bath (p. 25).

3. In a medium-sized saucepan, combine cream, milk, 1 cup (236 ml) bourbon cherries, sugar and salt. Using an immersion blender, purée until smooth. (Or you can blend ingredients in a regular blender, then transfer to a saucepan.) Stir over medium-high heat for about 5 minutes, until steam begins to rise from the surface. Remove from heat.

4. While the dairy is warming, whisk the egg yolks in a medium-sized bowl. To temper the yolks, slowly pour 1 cup of the heated cream mixture into the yolks while whisking vigorously. Continue adding heated cream and whisking until about half of the hot cream has been added. Transfer the yolk mixture to the pan.

5. Cook the mixture over medium heat, stirring continuously with a heatproof spatula, until the mixture is thick enough to coat the spatula or a digital thermometer reads 180°F (about 5–6 minutes). Immediately remove from heat and strain the custard through a fine-mesh sieve into the inner bowl of the prepared ice bath.

### BOURBON CHERRIES

3 cups (400 g) fresh black cherries (70–80 cherries), pitted

¼ cup (50 g) firmly packed light brown sugar

1 Tbsp water

2 Tbsp (30 ml) bourbon

### BOURBON CHERRY ICE CREAM

2 cups (473 ml) heavy cream

1 cup (236 ml) whole milk

1 qty Bourbon Cherries (see here), divided

½ cup (100 g) sugar

¼ tsp fine sea salt

5 large egg yolks (90 g)

1 Tbsp bourbon

6. Stir in bourbon. Cool the custard in the ice bath until room temperature, stirring occasionally. Cover and chill in the refrigerator for at least 4 hours, or overnight.

7. Place storage container in the freezer to chill. Freeze the mixture in an ice cream maker according to the manufacturer's instructions until ice cream is thick and creamy and has increased in volume by about a third.

8. Spoon a few scoops of just-churned ice cream into your storage container. Dollop some bourbon cherries on top. Using a butter knife, gently swirl the cherries into the ice cream. Repeat by layering with ice cream and the remaining bourbon cherries.

9. Enjoy immediately or freeze 2 hours for a firmer scoop. For storage tips see p. 28.

## BOOZE

When used in moderation, alcohol, with its low freezing point, can help you achieve a quintessential parlour-style scoop. Even if you're not looking for a booze-forward flavour, 1 tablespoon of a mildly flavoured alcohol can significantly help with scoopability. Adding more than 3 or 4 tablespoons of hard alcohol can make your ice cream too soft, or it can inhibit freezing all together—so be wary and follow the recipe. Alcohol should be added to the ice cream mixture only after the saucepan has been removed from the heat, otherwise it will cook off.

Bourbon Black Cherry
(p. 114)

Apple Pie
(p. 118)

What came first: ice cream or apple pie? We only know the two are inextricably and most agreeably linked. Around Thanksgiving, when Ontario apples are tumbling off the stands at the outdoor markets, we buy bushels and bake pies to churn into our frozen custard. For this recipe, we make a well-seasoned apple compote to fold into a cinnamon ice cream base.

# APPLE PIE

MAKES ABOUT 1 QUART

### APPLE PIE COMPOTE

1. In a medium-sized saucepan, melt butter and brown sugar over medium heat. Add apples, lemon juice, cinnamon, nutmeg and salt. Simmer for 10–12 minutes, stirring occasionally, until apples are tender and liquid is syrupy. Remove from heat and stir in vanilla. Set aside to cool.

   Compote can be stored in a sealed glass jar in the refrigerator for up to 2 weeks. Makes about ½ cup.

### APPLE PIE ICE CREAM

2. In a medium-sized saucepan, combine cream, milk, sugar, salt and cinnamon sticks. Stir over medium-high heat for about 5 minutes, until steam begins to rise from the surface. Remove from heat. Cover the pan and steep cinnamon sticks for 15 minutes.

3. Prepare an ice bath (p. 25).

4. Reheat the dairy mixture over medium-high heat for 3–5 minutes, or until steam begins to rise from the surface.

5. While the dairy is warming, whisk the egg yolks in a medium-sized bowl. To temper the yolks, slowly pour 1 cup of the heated cream mixture into the yolks while whisking vigorously. Continue adding heated cream and whisking until about half of the hot cream has been added. Transfer the yolk mixture to the pan.

### APPLE PIE COMPOTE

1 Tbsp unsalted butter, room temperature

¼ cup (50 g) firmly packed light brown sugar

2 baking apples such as Lobo, Granny Smith, Honeycrisp and/or McIntosh, peeled, cored and cut into ¼-inch cubes (2 cups/235 g)

1 tsp fresh lemon juice

1 tsp ground cinnamon

¼ tsp ground nutmeg

¼ tsp fine sea salt

¼ tsp pure vanilla extract

### APPLE PIE ICE CREAM

2 cups (473 ml) heavy cream

1 cup (236 ml) whole milk

½ cup (100 g) sugar

¼ tsp fine sea salt

2 cinnamon sticks, broken in half

5 large egg yolks (90 g)

1½ tsp pure vanilla extract

1 qty Apple Pie Compote (see here)

6.  Cook the mixture over medium heat, stirring continuously with a heatproof spatula, until the mixture is thick enough to coat the spatula or a digital thermometer reads 180°F (about 5-6 minutes). Immediately remove from heat and strain the custard through a fine-mesh sieve into the inner bowl of the prepared ice bath.

7.  Add the cinnamon sticks back into the mixture to intensify the cinnamon flavour. Stir in vanilla. Cool the custard in the ice bath until room temperature, stirring occasionally. Cover and chill in the refrigerator for at least 4 hours, or overnight.

8.  Remove and discard cinnamon sticks. Place storage container in the freezer to chill. Freeze the mixture in an ice cream maker according to the manufacturer's instructions until ice cream is thick and creamy and has increased in volume by about a third.

9.  Spoon a few scoops of just-churned ice cream into your storage container. Dollop some apple pie compote on top. Using a butter knife, gently swirl compote into the ice cream. Repeat by layering with ice cream and more compote.

10. Enjoy immediately or freeze 2 hours for a firmer scoop. For storage tips see p. 28.

All the deep sweet banana bread flavours are here in this ice cream, but with a boosted banana flavour thanks to the roasting of the fruit. The buttermilk in the base lends an elegant tang. Extremely ripe bananas produce the finest results.

# BANANA BREAD

MAKES ABOUT 1 QUART

### ROASTED BANANA PURÉE

1. Preheat oven to 400°F. Line a baking sheet with parchment paper.

2. Lay bananas in a single layer on the prepared baking sheet. Sprinkle brown sugar over bananas and drop dollops of butter evenly on top. Bake for 16–18 minutes, until bananas are deeply golden and edges turn dark.

3. Transfer warm bananas to a food processor. (We recommend placing one corner of the pan just inside the processor bowl and using a spatula to scrape in the bananas and any candied bits.) Pulse bananas until very smooth. You can use the warm bananas in the ice cream base immediately.

   If you're preparing purée for later use, cool completely and store in an airtight container in the refrigerator for up to 5 days. Makes about ¼ cup.

### BANANA BREAD ICE CREAM

4. Prepare an ice bath (p. 25).

5. In a medium-sized saucepan, combine banana purée, cream, buttermilk, milk, brown sugar, cinnamon and salt. Stir over medium-high heat for about 5 minutes, until steam begins to rise from the surface. Remove from heat.

6. While the dairy is warming, whisk the egg yolks in a medium-sized bowl. To temper the yolks, slowly pour 1 cup of the heated cream mixture into the yolks while whisking vigorously. Continue adding heated cream and whisking until about half of the hot cream has been added. Transfer the yolk mixture to the pan.

### ROASTED BANANA PURÉE

2 ripe bananas, sliced diagonally about ¼ inch thick

¼ cup (50 g) firmly packed light brown sugar

¼ cup (57 g) unsalted butter, room temperature

### BANANA BREAD ICE CREAM

1 qty Roasted Banana Purée (see here)

2 cups (473 ml) heavy cream

½ cup (118 ml) buttermilk (see Tip)

½ cup (118 ml) whole milk

½ cup (100 g) firmly packed light brown sugar

½ tsp ground cinnamon

¼ tsp fine sea salt

5 large egg yolks (90 g)

7. Cook the mixture over medium heat, stirring continuously with a heatproof spatula, until the mixture is thick enough to coat the spatula or a digital thermometer reads 180°F (about 5-6 minutes). Immediately remove from heat and strain the custard through a fine-mesh sieve into the inner bowl of the prepared ice bath, pressing down on any banana bits with a stiff rubber spatula to extract as much flavour as possible.

8. Cool the custard in the ice bath until room temperature, stirring occasionally. Cover and chill in the refrigerator for at least 4 hours, or overnight.

9. Place storage container in the freezer to chill. Freeze the mixture in an ice cream maker according to the manufacturer's instructions until ice cream is thick and creamy and has increased in volume by about a third.

10. Enjoy immediately or freeze 2 hours in chilled storage container for a firmer scoop. For storage tips see p. 28.

**HOMEMADE BUTTERMILK**

To make buttermilk, put ½ tablespoon of lemon juice in a liquid measuring cup. Pour in milk until the ½ cup measure is reached. Set aside the mixture for about 5 minutes, until curdled.

We love the balance of ultra-sweet white chocolate and sea salt in this recipe. We also love how the salt-sprinkled chocolate caramelizes and develops all those toasty aromas as it's slow-roasted in the oven. Be certain to source a high-quality white chocolate from a craft chocolate shop or specialty grocer.

# TOASTED WHITE CHOCOLATE & SEA SALT

**MAKES ABOUT 1 QUART**

### TOASTED WHITE CHOCOLATE

1. Preheat oven to 325°F. Line a baking sheet with parchment paper.

2. Spread chocolate on the prepared baking sheet in an even layer and sprinkle with salt. Bake for 6–8 minutes, or until chocolate turns golden brown. Agitate the chocolate with a heatproof spatula so it crumbles. (Yes, it will actually crumble!) Set aside to cool.

   Chocolate can be stored in an airtight container at room temperature for up to 3 days. Makes about ½ cup.

### TOASTED WHITE CHOCOLATE & SEA SALT ICE CREAM

3. Prepare an ice bath (p. 25).

4. In a medium-sized saucepan, combine cream, milk, sugar and salt. Stir over medium-high heat for about 5 minutes, until steam begins to rise from the surface. Remove from heat.

5. Add toasted chocolate, then use an immersion blender to blend until smooth. (Or you can blend ingredients in a regular blender. Remove the filler cap and cover with a tea towel to avoid a mess when blending. Transfer to the saucepan.)

6. While the dairy is warming, whisk the egg yolks in a medium-sized bowl. To temper the yolks, slowly pour 1 cup of the heated cream mixture into the yolks while whisking vigorously. Continue adding heated cream and whisking until about half of the hot cream has been added. Transfer the yolk mixture to the pan.

### TOASTED WHITE CHOCOLATE

1 cup (160 g) chopped white chocolate, with at least 28% cocoa butter

½ tsp flaky sea salt

### TOASTED WHITE CHOCOLATE & SEA SALT ICE CREAM

2 cups (473 ml) heavy cream

1 cup (236 ml) whole milk

½ cup (100 g) sugar

½ tsp fine sea salt

½ cup (160 g) Toasted White Chocolate (see here)

5 large egg yolks (90 g)

7. Cook the mixture over medium heat, stirring continuously with a heatproof spatula, until the mixture is thick enough to coat the spatula or a digital thermometer reads 180°F (about 5-6 minutes). Immediately remove from heat and strain the custard through a fine-mesh sieve into the inner bowl of the prepared ice bath.

8. Cool the custard in the ice bath until room temperature, stirring occasionally. Cover and chill in the refrigerator for at least 4 hours, or overnight.

9. Place storage container in the freezer to chill. Freeze the mixture in an ice cream maker according to the manufacturer's instructions until ice cream is thick and creamy and has increased in volume by about a third.

10. Enjoy immediately or freeze 2 hours in chilled storage container for a firmer scoop. For storage tips see p. 28.

**WHITE CHOCOLATE 2.0**

To create an intense caramelized flavour, bake the white chocolate in an oven preheated to 250°F, for a total of 35-40 minutes, stirring every 10 minutes, until golden. The chocolate will be crumbly at first, then caramelize and melt as it bakes. Proceed with recipe while chocolate is still warm and fluid.

With Little Italy as our neighbour, we celebrate the annual Italian Week festival by turning our entire ice cream cabinet into one of Italian-inspired flavours. Our tiramisu incorporates all the essential elements of Italy's most famous dessert—silky mascarpone cheese, strong espresso, cocoa powder, ladyfingers and a dash of a coffee liqueur—churned into a luscious ice cream dessert.

# TIRAMISU

GLUTEN   MAKES ABOUT 1 QUART

### LADYFINGERS

1. Combine espresso and coffee liqueur in a shallow dish. Dip ladyfingers for 2 seconds on each side before removing. Chop lady fingers into ½-inch pieces and freeze in a single layer on a baking sheet.

   Frozen ladyfinger pieces can be stored in an airtight container in the freezer for up to 2 weeks. Makes about ½ cup.

### TIRAMISU ICE CREAM

2. Prepare an ice bath (p. 25).

3. In a medium-sized saucepan, whisk mascarpone, cream, milk, sugar, espresso and salt. Stir over medium-high heat for about 5 minutes, until steam begins to rise from the surface and mascarpone is incorporated. Remove from heat.

4. While the dairy is warming, whisk the egg yolks in a medium-sized bowl. To temper the yolks, slowly pour 1 cup of the heated cream mixture into the yolks while whisking vigorously. Continue adding heated cream and whisking until about half of the hot cream has been added. Transfer the yolk mixture to the pan.

5. Cook the mixture over medium heat, stirring continuously with a heatproof spatula, until the mixture is thick enough to coat the spatula or a digital thermometer reads 180°F (about 5–6 minutes). Immediately remove from heat and strain the custard through a fine-mesh sieve into the inner bowl of the prepared ice bath.

### LADYFINGERS

¼ cup (59 ml) espresso

2 Tbsp (30 ml) coffee liqueur

6 ladyfingers

### TIRAMISU ICE CREAM

1 cup (236 g) mascarpone

1 cup (236 ml) heavy cream

1 cup (236 ml) whole milk

½ cup (100 g) sugar

2 Tbsp (30 ml) espresso

¼ tsp fine sea salt

5 large egg yolks (90 g)

2 Tbsp (30 ml) coffee liqueur

1 qty Ladyfingers (see here)

Dutch-processed cocoa powder, for dusting

6. Stir in coffee liqueur. Cool the custard in the ice bath until room temperature, stirring occasionally. Cover and chill in the refrigerator for at least 4 hours, or overnight.

7. Place storage container in the freezer to chill. Freeze the mixture in an ice cream maker according to the manufacturer's instructions until ice cream is thick and creamy and has increased in volume by about a third.

8. Once churned, add in ladyfingers and churn for a further 30 seconds until incorporated.

9. Enjoy immediately or freeze 2 hours in chilled storage container for a firmer scoop. Serve each scoop with a dusting of cocoa. For storage tips see p. 28.

**BOOZE**

When used in moderation, alcohol, with its low freezing point, can help you achieve a quintessential parlour-style scoop. Even if you're not looking for a booze-forward flavour, 1 tablespoon of a mildly flavoured alcohol can significantly help with scoopability. Adding more than 3 or 4 tablespoons of hard alcohol can make your ice cream too soft, or it can inhibit freezing all together—so be wary and follow the recipe. Alcohol should be added to the ice cream mixture only after the saucepan has been removed from the heat, otherwise it will cook off.

Tiramisu
(p. 124)

Sugar-Plumped Fig & Earl Grey
(p. 128)

Marlene's sister claims she would make the five-hour drive from her home in Guelph just for a scoop of this. Although she knows we'd give her an extra big one for her troubles... This flavour starts with cooking dried figs in a sugar syrup to fatten them up before dropping them in the Earl Grey–infused base. A high-quality, bergamot-forward tea is key.

# SUGAR-PLUMPED FIG & EARL GREY

VEGAN   MAKES ABOUT 1 QUART

### SUGAR-PLUMPED FIGS

1. Combine sugar and water in a small saucepan and bring to a boil over high heat. Remove from heat and stir in figs. Set aside for 20 minutes.

2. Using a fine-mesh sieve, drain figs and set aside to cool. (The syrup makes a beautiful sweetener for teas and cocktails. Store in a sealed glass jar in the refrigerator for up to 1 month.)

   Figs can be stored in an airtight container in the refrigerator for up to 2 weeks. Makes about ½ cup.

### SUGAR-PLUMPED FIG & EARL GREY ICE CREAM

3. Scoop out 1½ cups (350 g) coconut cream from the chilled cans of coconut milk and reserve coconut water for another use. Whisk together coconut cream, coconut milk, sugar and salt in a medium-sized saucepan. Stir for 5–7 minutes over medium-high heat, until sugar is dissolved and no visible bits of coconut cream remain. Reduce heat to low and add tea. Steep for 20 minutes.

4. While mixture is steeping, prepare an ice bath (p. 25).

5. After 20 minutes of steeping, remove mixture from heat and strain through a fine-mesh sieve into the inner bowl of the prepared ice bath, pressing down on the tea leaves with a stiff rubber spatula to extract as much flavour as possible.

### SUGAR-PLUMPED FIGS

1 cup (200 g) sugar

1 cup (236 ml) water

½ cup (80 g) dried figs, finely chopped

### SUGAR-PLUMPED FIG & EARL GREY ICE CREAM

2 (400 ml) cans coconut milk, chilled for 24 hours

1 (400 ml) can coconut milk, room temperature

1½ cups (300 g) sugar

¼ tsp fine sea salt

¼ cup (24 g) Earl Grey tea leaves

1 qty Sugar-Plumped Figs (see here)

6. Cool the ice cream base in the ice bath until room temperature. Chill overnight in the refrigerator.

7. Once the base is chilled, you may notice a layer of solids on the top. Give it all a quick mix to incorporate before churning. Place storage container in the freezer to chill. Freeze the mixture in an ice cream maker according to the manufacturer's instructions until ice cream is thick and creamy and has increased in volume by about a third. The base is ready when (with the machine turned off) you can scoop a big spoon of it and watch the ice cream fall back into the bowl in thick trails.

8. Once churned, add in sugar-plumped figs and churn for 30 seconds until incorporated.

9. Enjoy immediately or freeze 2 hours in chilled storage container for a firmer scoop. For storage tips see p. 28.

### TURN UP THE TEA

For a stronger tea flavour, add 2 teaspoons of tea leaves to the ice cream base after straining it. The leaves will continue to steep in the hot base and during the chill time, intensifying the flavour. Strain the base before churning.

This flavour reminds us of after-school snacks of nubbly cinnamon sugar on buttered fingers of toast—it has all the soft, sweet warmth of cinnamon wrapped in a pure, cold treat. Roasting the cinnamon-sugar butter creates candy-like clusters, which interrupt the smooth custard in delightful ways. This flavour is a splendid topper for apple pie, apple crumble, apple cake... or your Thanksgiving pumpkin pie.

# CINNAMON SUGAR

MAKES ABOUT 1 QUART

### CINNAMON SUGAR

1. Preheat oven to 325°F. Line a baking sheet with parchment paper.

2. In a small bowl, combine cinnamon and sugar. Using your fingertips, rub butter into cinnamon sugar until sandy.

3. Scatter cinnamon sugar in a single layer on the prepared baking sheet and bake for 5-6 minutes, until fragrant and darker. Set aside to cool completely, then break up any large clumps of cinnamon sugar.

   Cinnamon sugar can be stored in an airtight container at room temperature for up to 3 days. Makes about ½ cup.

### CINNAMON SUGAR ICE CREAM

4. In a medium-sized saucepan, combine cream, milk, sugar, cinnamon sticks and salt. Stir over medium-high heat for about 5 minutes, until steam begins to rise from the surface. Remove from heat. Cover and steep for 35 minutes.

5. Reheat the mixture over medium-high heat for 3-5 minutes, or until steam begins to rise from the surface.

6. Prepare an ice bath (p. 25).

7. While the dairy is warming, whisk the egg yolks in a medium-sized bowl. To temper the yolks, slowly pour 1 cup of the heated cream mixture into the yolks while whisking vigorously. Continue adding heated cream and whisking until about half of the hot cream has been added. Transfer the yolk mixture to the pan.

### CINNAMON SUGAR

1 Tbsp ground cinnamon

¼ cup (50 g) sugar

1 Tbsp unsalted butter, room temperature

### CINNAMON SUGAR ICE CREAM

2 cups (473 ml) heavy cream

1 cup (236 ml) whole milk

½ cup (100 g) sugar

6 cinnamon sticks, broken in half

¼ tsp fine sea salt

5 large egg yolks (90 g)

½ cup (65 g) Cinnamon Sugar (see here)

8. Cook the mixture over medium heat, stirring continuously with a heatproof spatula, until the mixture is thick enough to coat the spatula or a digital thermometer reads 180°F (about 5-6 minutes). Immediately remove from heat and strain the custard through a fine-mesh sieve into the inner bowl of the prepared ice bath.

9. Add the cinnamon sticks back into the mixture to intensify the cinnamon flavour. Cool the custard in the ice bath until room temperature, stirring occasionally. Cover and chill in the refrigerator for at least 4 hours, or overnight.

10. Discard the cinnamon sticks. Place storage container in the freezer to chill. Freeze the mixture in an ice cream maker according to the manufacturer's instructions until ice cream is thick and creamy and has increased in volume by about a third.

11. Once churned, add in cinnamon sugar and churn for a further 30 seconds until incorporated.

12. Enjoy immediately or freeze 2 hours in chilled storage container for a firmer scoop. For storage tips see p. 28.

There's so much right about this flavour: chewy bits of brownie, ribbons of dulce de leche sauce and a sweetened coconut milk to ramp up the dark, deep caramel notes in the vegan ice cream base.

# DULCE DE LECHE BROWNIE BATTER

VEGAN / GLUTEN (OPTIONAL)    MAKES ABOUT 1 QUART

### COCONUT DULCE DE LECHE

1. Combine ingredients in a medium-sized saucepan. Bring to a boil over medium heat and cook for 20 minutes, stirring every 2–3 minutes, until thick and golden. Set aside to cool.

   Dulce de leche can be stored in a sealed glass jar in the refrigerator for up to 2 weeks. Makes about 1 cup.

### BROWNIE BATTER

2. In a small saucepan, melt maple syrup and coconut oil over low heat, stirring frequently. Stir in vanilla.

3. Add cocoa, flour and salt, and whisk to incorporate. Stir in chocolate chips.

   Brownie batter can be stored in an airtight container in the refrigerator for up to 4 days. Makes about ½ cup.

### DULCE DE LECHE ICE CREAM

4. Prepare an ice bath (p. 25).

5. Scoop out 1½ cups (350 g) coconut cream from the chilled cans of coconut milk and reserve coconut water for another use. Whisk together coconut cream, coconut milk, brown sugar, ½ cup (118 ml) coconut dulce de leche and salt in a medium-sized saucepan. Heat the mixture over medium-high heat for 5–7 minutes, until sugar is dissolved and no visible bits of coconut cream remain. Remove from heat and strain through a fine-mesh sieve into the inner bowl of the prepared ice bath.

6. Cool the ice cream base in the ice bath until room temperature, stirring occasionally. Cover and chill in the refrigerator for at least 4 hours, or overnight.

### COCONUT DULCE DE LECHE

1 (400 ml) can coconut milk, room temperature

¾ cup (150 g) firmly packed light brown sugar

¼ tsp fine sea salt

### BROWNIE BATTER

1 Tbsp pure maple syrup

1 Tbsp coconut oil

½ tsp pure vanilla extract

1 Tbsp Dutch-processed cocoa powder

3 Tbsp (23 g) all-purpose flour or gluten-free flour blend, heat treated (see Tip)

¼ tsp fine sea salt

2 Tbsp (23 g) mini chocolate chips

7. Once the base is chilled, you may notice a layer of solids on the top. Give it all a quick mix to incorporate before churning. Place storage container in the freezer to chill. Freeze the mixture in an ice cream maker according to the manufacturer's instructions until ice cream is thick and creamy and has increased in volume by about a third. The base is ready when (with the machine turned off) you can scoop a big spoon of it and watch the ice cream fall back into the bowl in thick trails.

8. While the ice cream is churning, use a teaspoon to portion out the brownie batter into balls. Once churned, add in brownie batter and churn for a further 30 seconds until incorporated. Spoon a few scoops of just-churned ice cream into your storage container. Dollop some dulce de leche on top. Using a butter knife, gently swirl the dulce de leche into the ice cream. Repeat by layering with ice cream and more dulce de leche.

9. Enjoy immediately or freeze 2 hours for a firmer scoop. For storage tips see p. 28.

**DULCE DE LECHE ICE CREAM**

2 (400 ml) cans coconut milk, chilled for 24 hours

1 (400 ml) can coconut milk, room temperature

1 cup (200 g) firmly packed light brown sugar

1 qty Coconut Dulce de Leche (see here), divided

¼ tsp fine sea salt

½ cup (92 g) Brownie Batter (see here)

---

**HEAT-TREATING FLOUR**

Flours are made from raw grains, and the milling process does not kill bacteria. To heat-treat flour, scatter it on a baking sheet, then bake for 5 minutes in a 350°F oven. Cool the flour, sift, then proceed with the recipe.

Dulce de Leche Brownie Batter
(p. 132)

Toasting all the wonderful spices—cloves, cardamom, cinnamon and the many other fragrant seeds and pods and berries that together create the fragrance of a great Masala chai—will make a world of difference to the flavour of this ice cream (see Tip). And your kitchen will smell fabulous too!

# CHAI LATTE

MAKES ABOUT 1 QUART

1. In a medium-sized saucepan, combine cream, milk, sugar, salt and spices. Stir over medium-high heat for about 5 minutes, until steam begins to rise from the surface. Remove from heat, cover and steep for 1 hour.

2. Reheat mixture over medium-high heat for 5 minutes, or when steam rises from the surface. Add tea leaves. Remove from heat, cover and steep for 15 minutes.

3. Prepare an ice bath (p. 25).

4. Reheat the mixture over medium-high heat for 3–5 minutes, or until steam begins to rise from the surface.

5. While the dairy is warming, whisk the egg yolks in a medium-sized bowl. To temper the yolks, slowly pour 1 cup of the heated cream mixture into the yolks while whisking vigorously. Continue adding heated cream and whisking until about half of the hot cream has been added. Transfer the yolk mixture to the pan.

6. Cook the mixture over medium heat, stirring continuously with a heatproof spatula, until the mixture is thick enough to coat the spatula or a digital thermometer reads 180°F (about 5-6 minutes). Immediately remove from heat and strain the custard through a fine-mesh sieve into the inner bowl of the prepared ice bath.

7. Cool the custard in the ice bath until room temperature, stirring occasionally. Cover and chill in the refrigerator for at least 4 hours, or overnight.

8. Place storage container in the freezer to chill. Freeze the mixture in an ice cream maker according to the manufacturer's instructions until ice cream is thick and creamy and has increased in volume by about a third.

9. Enjoy immediately or freeze 2 hours in chilled storage container for a firmer scoop. For storage tips see p. 28.

2 cups (473 ml) heavy cream

1 cup (236 ml) whole milk

½ cup (100 g) sugar

¼ tsp fine sea salt

10 cloves, toasted

10 whole allspice berries, toasted

4 cardamom pods, crushed and toasted

4 whole black peppercorns, toasted

2 cinnamon sticks, toasted

2 star anise, toasted

1 Tbsp grated ginger

1 tsp coriander seeds, toasted

¼ cup (24 g) black tea leaves

5 large egg yolks (90 g)

### HOW TO TOAST SPICES

To toast spices, set a medium-sized pan over medium heat. Scatter spices in a single layer and toast, stirring often, until spices are very fragrant and start to pop.

Noble livestock champions, record-holding pumpkin pie competitions, apple pie bake-offs and buckets of caramel corn. This flavour is an ode to the fall fairs of our childhoods, such a huge part of our Canadian farm-girl lives. And in case you think popcorn will turn into a soggy disaster in a scoop of ice cream, let us assure you that its caramel coating acts as a beautiful barrier. We think this recipe would win us the blue ribbon for sure.

# CARAMEL POPCORN

MAKES ABOUT 1 QUART

### CARAMEL-COVERED POPCORN

1. Line a baking sheet with parchment paper. Add popcorn to a medium-sized bowl and set aside.

2. Melt butter and brown sugar in a small saucepan over medium heat. Bring to a boil, then boil for precisely 2 minutes. Stir in salt, vanilla and baking soda. Drizzle caramel over the popcorn and stir well to coat.

3. Scatter caramel popcorn over the prepared baking sheet and set aside for 10 minutes, or until set.

   Popcorn can be stored in an airtight container for up to 1 week. Makes about 1 cup.

### BUTTERED POPCORN ICE CREAM

4. In a medium-sized saucepan, combine cream, milk, sugar, popcorn and salt. Stir over medium-high heat for about 5 minutes, until steam begins to rise from the surface. Remove from heat. Cover and steep for 30 minutes.

5. Prepare an ice bath (p. 25).

6. Reheat the mixture over medium heat for 5 minutes, or until steam begins to rise from the surface.

7. While the dairy is warming, whisk the egg yolks in a medium-sized bowl. To temper the yolks, slowly pour 1 cup of the heated cream mixture into the yolks while whisking vigorously. Continue adding heated cream and whisking until about half of the hot cream has been added. Transfer the yolk mixture to the pan.

### CARAMEL-COVERED POPCORN

1 cup (10 g) popped, buttered and salted popcorn

2 Tbsp (28 g) unsalted butter

2 Tbsp (25 g) light brown sugar

⅛ tsp fine sea salt

¼ tsp pure vanilla extract

¼ tsp baking soda

### BUTTERED POPCORN ICE CREAM

2 cups (473 ml) heavy cream

1 cup (236 ml) whole milk

½ cup (100 g) sugar

2 cups (20 g) popped, buttered and salted popcorn

¼ tsp fine sea salt

5 large egg yolks (90 g)

1 qty Caramel-Covered Popcorn (see here), broken into small pieces

8.  Cook the mixture over medium heat, stirring continuously with a heatproof spatula, until the mixture is thick enough to coat the spatula or a digital thermometer reads 180°F (about 5-6 minutes). Immediately remove from heat and strain the custard through a fine-mesh sieve into the inner bowl of the prepared ice bath, pressing down on the popcorn bits with a stiff rubber spatula to extract as much flavour as possible.

9.  Cool the custard in the ice bath until room temperature, stirring occasionally. Cover and chill in the refrigerator for at least 4 hours, or overnight.

10. Place storage container in the freezer to chill. Freeze the mixture in an ice cream maker according to the manufacturer's instructions until ice cream is thick and creamy and has increased in volume by about a third.

11. Once churned, add in caramel popcorn and churn for another for 30 seconds until incorporated.

12. Enjoy immediately or freeze 2 hours in chilled storage container for a firmer scoop. For storage tips see p. 28.

There's a wintry nip in the air as we rake the fall leaves, and we find ourselves longing for rich, sticky foods. It's the perfect time for this ice cream, which takes our 24-carat Brown-Butter Brownies (p. 203) and suspends them in coffee ice cream. Even when frozen, the brownie bits remain chewy, fudgy and ... gold.

# COFFEE FUDGE BROWNIE

GLUTEN (OPTIONAL)   MAKES ABOUT 1 QUART

1. Prepare an ice bath (p. 25).

2. In a medium-sized saucepan, combine cream, milk, sugar, freeze-dried coffee, cocoa and salt. Stir over medium-high heat for about 5 minutes, until steam begins to rise from the surface. Remove from heat.

3. While the dairy is warming, whisk the egg yolks in a medium-sized bowl. To temper the yolks, slowly pour 1 cup of the heated cream mixture into the yolks while whisking vigorously. Continue adding heated cream and whisking until about half of the hot cream has been added. Transfer the yolk mixture to the pan.

4. Cook the mixture over medium heat, stirring continuously with a heatproof spatula, until the mixture is thick enough to coat the spatula or a digital thermometer reads 180°F (about 5–6 minutes). Immediately remove from heat and strain the custard through a fine-mesh sieve into the inner bowl of the prepared ice bath.

5. Cool the custard in the ice bath until room temperature, stirring occasionally. Cover and chill in the refrigerator for at least 4 hours, or overnight.

6. Place storage container in the freezer to chill. Freeze the mixture in an ice cream maker according to the manufacturer's instructions until ice cream is thick and creamy and has increased in volume by about a third.

7. Once churned, add in brownie pieces and churn for 30 seconds until incorporated.

8. Enjoy immediately or freeze 2 hours in chilled storage container for a firmer scoop. For storage tips see p. 28.

2 cups (473 ml) heavy cream

1 cup (236 ml) whole milk

½ cup (100 g) sugar

2 Tbsp (10 g) freeze-dried coffee (see Tip)

1 tsp Dutch-processed cocoa powder

¼ tsp fine sea salt

5 large egg yolks (90 g)

1½ cups (220 g) Brown-Butter Brownies (p. 203), cut into bite-sized pieces

**FREEZE-DRIED COFFEE SWAP**

In place of freeze-dried coffee, whole coffee beans can be steeped in the cream base (for about 1 hour) before the eggs are added, though the coffee flavour will be more muted.

Who knew that one of life's most fantastic combinations is sea salt and caramel? This flavour is never left off our menu board. If it were, our merry heads would roll. The salted caramel sauce is so good, people are always asking us to bottle it. We sometimes even oblige!

# SALTED CARAMEL

MAKES ABOUT 1 QUART

1. Prepare an ice bath (p. 25).

2. Combine cream, milk and 1 cup salted caramel sauce in a medium-sized saucepan. Stir over medium-high heat for about 5 minutes, until steam begins to rise from the surface. Remove from heat.

3. While the dairy is warming, whisk the egg yolks in a medium-sized bowl. To temper the yolks, slowly pour 1 cup of the heated cream mixture into the yolks while whisking vigorously. Continue adding heated cream and whisking until about half of the hot cream has been added. Transfer the yolk mixture to the pan.

4. Cook the mixture over medium heat, stirring continuously with a heatproof spatula, until the mixture is thick enough to coat the spatula or a digital thermometer reads 180°F (about 5–6 minutes). Immediately remove from heat and strain the custard through a fine-mesh sieve into the inner bowl of the prepared ice bath.

5. Stir in vanilla. Cool the custard in the ice bath until room temperature, stirring occasionally. Cover and chill in the refrigerator for at least 4 hours, or overnight.

6. Place storage container in the freezer to chill. Freeze the mixture in an ice cream maker according to the manufacturer's instructions until ice cream is thick and creamy and has increased in volume by about a third.

7. Spoon a few scoops of just-churned ice cream into your storage container. Dollop some caramel sauce on top. Using a butter knife, gently swirl sauce into ice cream. Repeat by layering with ice cream and more sauce.

8. Enjoy immediately or freeze 2 hours for a firmer scoop. For storage tips see p. 28.

2 cups (473 ml) heavy cream

1 cup (236 ml) whole milk

1¼ cups (295 ml) Salted Caramel Sauce (p. 198), divided

5 large egg yolks (90 g)

½ tsp pure vanilla extract

---

### HARDENED SUGAR

Did the sugar harden in your saucepan? Don't fret! Fill the saucepan with water and bring to a boil. By the time the water boils, most of the candy will be dissolved.

This recipe is for our grandfathers, who loved nothing more than a wee dram enjoyed with a wee scoop, preferably by a fire. We don't soak the oak chips, as you might for your barbecue or smoker. The goal is to get some colour on them and then have that colour transfer to the cream. But watch them carefully so they don't burn—as you enjoy the marvellous scent of forest in your kitchen.

# TOASTED OAK & WHISKEY CARAMEL

MAKES ABOUT 1 QUART

### WHISKEY CARAMEL

1. In a medium-sized saucepan, gently stir sugar, corn syrup, water and salt. Attach a candy thermometer to the pan. Make sure the tip of the thermometer is fully submerged but does not touch the bottom of the pan, to ensure an accurate reading. Bring the mixture to a boil over high heat.

2. Place measured butter and cream next to the stove. Keep an oven mitt (to protect your mixing hand from hot steam) and whisk nearby.

3. Cook for 3–4 minutes, until sugar is deep copper, smells nutty and the thermometer reads between 375°F and 380°F. Remove from heat. Gingerly add butter from a low height, being sure not to splash sugar upward. Put on an oven mitt and whisk vigorously. The mixture will billow up, then settle down. Stream in cream and whisk until bubbling has subsided. If there are clumps of caramel, cook on low heat until the clumps have dissolved. Whisk in whiskey.

4. Set pan aside for 10 minutes to cool. If not using right away transfer sauce to a glass jar to fully cool. The sauce will thicken as it cools.

   Caramel can be stored at room temperature for up to 1 month or in the refrigerator for up to 2 months. Makes about ½ cup.

### TOASTED OAK & WHISKEY CARAMEL ICE CREAM

5. Place oak chips in a medium-sized saucepan and stir over medium-high heat for 4–6 minutes, until very fragrant and toasted. Add cream, milk, sugar and salt to the pan and stir for 5 minutes, or until steam begins to rise from the surface. Remove from heat. Cover and steep for 30 minutes.

**WHISKEY CARAMEL**

½ cup (100 g) sugar

1 Tbsp corn syrup

2 Tbsp (30 ml) water

⅛ tsp fine sea salt

1 Tbsp unsalted butter

2 Tbsp (30 ml) heavy cream

2 Tbsp (30 ml) whiskey

**TOASTED OAK & WHISKEY CARAMEL ICE CREAM**

½ cup (30 g) oak wood chips from a wine/beer supply store

2 cups (473 ml) heavy cream

1 cup (236 ml) whole milk

½ cup (100 g) sugar

¼ tsp fine sea salt

5 large egg yolks (90 g)

1 qty Whiskey Caramel (see here)

6. Reheat the mixture over medium-high heat for 3-5 minutes, or until steam begins to rise from the surface.

7. Prepare an ice bath (p. 25).

8. While the dairy is warming, whisk the egg yolks in a medium-sized bowl. To temper the yolks, slowly pour 1 cup of the heated cream mixture into the yolks while whisking vigorously. Continue adding heated cream and whisking until about half of the hot cream has been added. Transfer the yolk mixture to the pan.

9. Cook the mixture over medium heat, stirring continuously with a heatproof spatula, until the mixture is thick enough to coat the spatula or a digital thermometer reads 180°F (about 5-6 minutes). Immediately remove from heat and strain the custard through a fine-mesh sieve into the inner bowl of the prepared ice bath.

10. Cool the custard in the ice bath until room temperature, stirring occasionally. Cover and chill in the refrigerator for at least 4 hours, or overnight.

11. Place storage container in the freezer to chill. Freeze the mixture in an ice cream maker according to the manufacturer's instructions until ice cream is thick and creamy and has increased in volume by about a third.

12. While the ice cream is churning, warm the caramel in a small saucepan over low heat until very fluid but not hot. Spoon a few scoops of just-churned ice cream into your storage container. Dollop some caramel on top. Using a butter knife, gently swirl the caramel into the ice cream. Repeat by layering with the remaining ice cream and caramel sauce.

13. Enjoy immediately or freeze 2 hours for a firmer scoop. For storage tips see p. 28.

**A CHEWIER SWIRL**

For a chewier swirl, increase the amount of fat by adding an additional 1 tablespoon of butter to the pan with the cream.

# WINTER

Freshly grated nutmeg is key in this eggnog ice cream. Oh yes, and a splash of brandy. That's key too, for a Christmas Eve flavour and to slice through the ultra-rich base. As with all recipes that incorporate alcohol, don't take liberties with the amount stated in the recipe or your ice cream may not freeze. You're better to have a glass of brandy on the side.

# MERRY EGGNOG

MAKES ABOUT 1 QUART

1. Prepare an ice bath (p. 25).

2. In a medium-sized saucepan, combine cream, milk, sugar and salt. Stir over medium-high heat for about 5 minutes, until steam begins to rise from the surface. Remove from heat.

3. While the dairy is warming, whisk the egg yolks in a medium-sized bowl. To temper the yolks, slowly pour 1 cup of the heated cream mixture into the yolks while whisking vigorously. Continue adding heated cream and whisking until about half of the hot cream has been added. Transfer the yolk mixture to the pan.

4. Cook the mixture over medium heat, stirring continuously with a heatproof spatula, until the mixture is thick enough to coat the spatula or a digital thermometer reads 180°F (about 5–6 minutes). Immediately remove from heat and strain the custard through a fine-mesh sieve into the inner bowl of the prepared ice bath.

5. Stir in nutmeg, brandy and vanilla. Cool the custard in the ice bath until room temperature, stirring occasionally. Cover and chill in the refrigerator for at least 4 hours, or overnight.

6. Place storage container in the freezer to chill. Freeze the mixture in an ice cream maker according to the manufacturer's instructions until ice cream is thick and creamy and has increased in volume by about a third.

7. Enjoy immediately or freeze 2 hours in chilled storage container for a firmer scoop. For storage tips see p. 28.

2 cups (473 ml) heavy cream

1 cup (236 ml) whole milk

½ cup (100 g) sugar

¼ tsp fine sea salt

6 large egg yolks (108 g)

1 tsp ground nutmeg

3 Tbsp (45 ml) brandy

2 tsp pure vanilla extract

### BOOZE

When used in moderation, alcohol, with its low freezing point, can help you achieve a quintessential parlour-style scoop. Even if you're not looking for a booze-forward flavour, 1 tablespoon of a mildly flavoured alcohol can significantly help with scoopability. Adding more than 3 or 4 tablespoons of hard alcohol can make your ice cream too soft, or it can inhibit freezing all together—so be wary and follow the recipe. Alcohol should be added to the ice cream mixture only after the saucepan has been removed from the heat, otherwise it will cook off.

When winter citrus is about the only fruit worth eating during our deep dark Canadian winter, we buy them all—grapefruits, navel oranges, clementines, mandarins, blood oranges, lemons, limes, pomelos—and toss their zests into our coconut-milk base. Use whatever citrus looks good to you and don't strain this one—you want the zest in the ice cream. (More vitamin C! And it looks so pretty.)

# COCONUT CITRUS BURST

**VEGAN**   **MAKES ABOUT 1 QUART**

1. Prepare an ice bath (p. 25).

2. Put sugar and citrus zest in a medium-sized bowl. Using your fingers, massage sugar into zest until no clumps of zest remain. The jagged edge of the sugar will aggravate the zest, causing it to release more oils—which results in more flavour.

3. Scoop out 1½ cups (350 g) coconut cream from the chilled cans of coconut milk and reserve coconut water for another use. Whisk together coconut cream, coconut milk, citrus juice, sugar mixture and salt in a medium-sized saucepan. Stir over medium-high heat for 5-7 minutes, until sugar is dissolved and no visible bits of coconut cream remain. Remove from heat and pour into the inner bowl of the prepared ice bath.

4. Cool the ice cream base in the ice bath until room temperature, stirring occasionally. Cover and chill in the refrigerator for at least 4 hours, or overnight.

5. Once the base is chilled, you may notice a layer of solids on the top. Give it all a quick mix to incorporate before churning. Place storage container in the freezer to chill. Freeze the mixture in an ice cream maker according to the manufacturer's instructions until ice cream is thick and creamy and has increased in volume by about a third. The base is ready when (with the machine turned off) you can scoop a big spoon of it and watch the ice cream fall back into the bowl in thick trails.

6. Enjoy immediately or freeze 2 hours in chilled storage container for a firmer scoop. For storage tips see p. 28.

1½ cups (300 g) sugar

3 Tbsp (18 g) packed citrus zest

2 (400 ml) cans coconut milk, chilled for 24 hours

1 (400 ml) can coconut milk, room temperature

½ cup (118 ml) citrus juice

¼ tsp fine sea salt

When our produce shops are heavy with sunny oranges, we crank up the tunes and have a zesting party. And then we churn this sophisticated flavour with a cold-pressed, extra-virgin olive oil by our friends at Il Negozio Nicastro, a local Italian deli. A high-quality oil is key to this ice cream's luscious flavour. Top a scoop with roasted fruit or serve with a slice of olive oil cake for a lovely dessert.

# OLIVE OIL & ORANGE

MAKES ABOUT 1 QUART

1. Prepare an ice bath (p. 25).

2. In a medium-sized saucepan, combine cream, milk, sugar, olive oil, orange juice, 2 tablespoons orange zest and salt. Stir over medium-high heat for about 5 minutes, until steam begins to rise from the surface. Remove from heat.

3. While the dairy is warming, whisk the egg yolks in a medium-sized bowl. To temper the yolks, slowly pour 1 cup of the heated cream mixture into the yolks while whisking vigorously. Continue adding heated cream and whisking until about half of the hot cream has been added. Transfer the yolk mixture to the pan.

4. Cook the mixture over medium heat, stirring continuously with a heatproof spatula, until the mixture is thick enough to coat the spatula or a digital thermometer reads 180°F (about 5–6 minutes). Immediately remove from heat and strain the custard through a fine-mesh sieve into the inner bowl of the prepared ice bath, pressing down on the orange zest with a stiff rubber spatula to extract as much flavour as possible.

5. Stir in the remaining 1 tablespoon of orange zest. Cool the custard in the ice bath until room temperature. Chill in the refrigerator for 4 hours, or overnight.

6. Place storage container in the freezer to chill. Freeze the mixture in an ice cream maker according to the manufacturer's instructions until ice cream is thick and creamy and has increased in volume by about a third.

7. Enjoy immediately or freeze 2 hours in chilled storage container for a firmer scoop. For storage tips see p. 28.

1½ cups (354 ml) heavy cream

1 cup (236 ml) whole milk

½ cup (100 g) sugar

½ cup (118 ml) high-quality extra-virgin olive oil

¼ cup (59 ml) fresh orange juice

3 Tbsp (18 g) packed navel orange zest, divided

¼ tsp fine sea salt

5 large egg yolks (90 g)

We use a rich cocoa powder, a dark chocolate bar and a handful of chocolate shards in this sensational recipe. The bar is hand-chopped—not our favourite task at The Merry Dairy—but it makes for different-sized shards, and those make for a more interesting ice cream. Buy the best-quality chocolate you can source and play around with a lighter or darker chocolate. For this recipe, we use a dark chocolate with 70-75% cocoa.

# TRIPLE CHOCOLATE

MAKES ABOUT 1 QUART

1. Prepare an ice bath (p. 25).

2. In a medium-sized saucepan, whisk cream, milk, sugar, salt and cocoa over medium-high heat. Stir for 5 minutes, or until steam begins to rise from the surface. Remove from heat. Add in half (a scant ¾ cup) of chopped chocolate and set aside for 1 minute, or until chocolate is significantly softened. Whisk to fully combine.

3. While the dairy is warming, whisk the egg yolks in a medium-sized bowl. To temper the yolks, slowly pour 1 cup of the heated cream mixture into the yolks while whisking vigorously. Continue adding heated cream and whisking until about half of the hot cream has been added. Transfer the yolk mixture to the pan.

4. Cook the mixture over medium heat, stirring continuously with a heatproof spatula, until the mixture is thick enough to coat the spatula or a digital thermometer reads 180°F (about 5-6 minutes). Immediately remove from heat and strain the custard through a fine-mesh sieve into the inner bowl of the prepared ice bath.

5. Stir in vanilla. Cool the custard in the ice bath until room temperature, stirring occasionally. Cover and chill in the refrigerator for at least 4 hours, or overnight.

6. Place storage container in the freezer to chill. Freeze the mixture in an ice cream maker according to the manufacturer's instructions until ice cream is thick and creamy and has increased in volume by about a third.

7. Once churned, add in the remaining chopped chocolate and churn for a further 30 seconds until incorporated.

8. Enjoy immediately or freeze 2 hours in chilled storage container for a firmer scoop. For storage tips see p. 28.

2 cups (473 ml) heavy cream

1 cup (236 ml) whole milk

½ cup (100 g) sugar

¼ tsp fine sea salt

⅓ cup (28 g) Dutch-processed cocoa powder

1⅓ cups (226 g) finely chopped dark chocolate (70-75% cocoa), divided

5 large egg yolks (90 g)

1 tsp pure vanilla extract

### HOW TO CHOP CHOCOLATE

A long, sharp serrated knife (think bread knife) works best for chopping chocolate. Cut the chocolate into thin shards by starting with the corner of a bar or block and rotating the bar as needed to chop from a corner or jutting edge.

Once we managed to source candy canes from a nut-free factory (no easy feat), and learned that extract of pure peppermint (and not one simply labelled "mint") is the way to keep ice cream from tasting like toothpaste, The Merry Dairy's dairy-free Peppermint Crackle became the season's bestseller.

# PEPPERMINT CRACKLE

**VEGAN**   **MAKES ABOUT 1 QUART**

1. Prepare an ice bath (p. 25).

2. Scoop out 1½ cups (350 g) coconut cream from the chilled cans of coconut milk and reserve coconut water for another use. Whisk together coconut cream, coconut milk, sugar and salt in a medium-sized saucepan. Heat the mixture over medium-high heat for 5–7 minutes, until sugar is dissolved and no visible bits of coconut cream remain. Remove from heat and strain through a fine-mesh sieve into the inner bowl of the prepared ice bath.

3. Stir in peppermint extract. Cool the ice cream base in the ice bath until room temperature, stirring occasionally. Cover and chill in the refrigerator for at least 4 hours, or overnight.

4. Once the base is chilled, you may notice a layer of solids on the top. Give it all a quick mix to incorporate before churning. Place storage container in the freezer to chill. Freeze the mixture in an ice cream maker according to the manufacturer's instructions until ice cream is thick and creamy and has increased in volume by about a third. The base is ready when (with the machine turned off) you can scoop a big spoon of it and watch the ice cream fall back into the bowl in thick trails.

5. While the ice cream is churning, make the crackle. In a small saucepan, melt chocolate and coconut oil over low heat, stirring frequently.

6. Once churned, add in candy cane. Stream in a tablespoon of chocolate and churn until incorporated then stream in a little more. If chocolate clumps to the paddle, stop churning and scrape down before continuing. Repeat until all the chocolate is used up.

7. Enjoy immediately or freeze 2 hours in chilled storage container for a firmer scoop. For storage tips see p. 28.

2 (400 ml) cans coconut milk, chilled for 24 hours

1 (400 ml) can coconut milk, room temperature

1½ cups (300 g) sugar

¼ tsp fine sea salt

4 tsp (20 ml) pure peppermint extract

¼ cup (45 g) coarsely chopped dark chocolate (70–75% cocoa)

1 tsp coconut oil

¼ cup (55 g) finely crushed candy cane (see Tip)

**CANDY CRUSH**

To crush candy canes, place them in a large resealable bag and seal tightly. Using a rolling pin, pound candies into small pieces.

**ADD-INS**

The chocolate should be heated only enough to stay fluid, and not any hotter. The coconut oil will cause the chocolate to seize as soon as it hits the semi-frozen ice cream.

A stunning vegan ice cream with all the aromatic spices and vibrant colour (and health-giving properties!) of hot turmeric milk or "golden milk" (also known in India as *haldi ka doodh*). As with any flavour calling for spices, the fresher the better. And you'll find giving the cinnamon sticks a quick toasting in a dry pan before adding them to the base to infuse lends a deeper flavour.

# GOLDEN MILK

VEGAN   MAKES ABOUT 1 QUART

1. Prepare an ice bath (p. 25).

2. Scoop out 1½ cups (350 g) coconut cream from the chilled cans of coconut milk and reserve coconut water for another use. Whisk together coconut cream, coconut milk, sugar, turmeric, ginger, cardamom, salt and pepper in a medium-sized saucepan. Stir over medium-high heat for 5-7 minutes, until sugar is dissolved and no visible bits of coconut cream remain.

3. Reduce heat to low, then add toasted cinnamon sticks and steep for 15 minutes, stirring occasionally. Remove from heat and strain through a fine-mesh sieve into the inner bowl of the prepared ice bath.

4. Stir in vanilla. Cool the ice cream base in the ice bath until room temperature, stirring occasionally. Cover and chill in the refrigerator for at least 4 hours, or overnight.

5. Once the base is chilled, you may notice a layer of solids on the top. Give it all a quick mix to incorporate before churning. Place storage container in the freezer to chill. Freeze the mixture in an ice cream maker according to the manufacturer's instructions until ice cream is thick and creamy and has increased in volume by about a third. The base is ready when (with the machine turned off) you can scoop a big spoon of it and watch the ice cream fall back into the bowl in thick trails.

6. Enjoy immediately or freeze 2 hours in chilled storage container for a firmer scoop. For storage tips see p. 28.

2 (400 ml) cans coconut milk, chilled for 24 hours

1 (400 ml) can coconut milk, room temperature

1½ cups (300 g) sugar

1 tsp ground turmeric

1 tsp ground ginger

¼ tsp ground cardamom

¼ tsp fine sea salt

⅛ tsp freshly ground black pepper

2 cinnamon sticks, toasted (see Tip, p. 135)

1 tsp pure vanilla extract

The goal with this ice cream was to make the flavour as close to that of a ginger cookie as we could manage, so we took all those lovely warm spices—ginger, cinnamon, cloves, nutmeg—along with molasses and brown sugar and tossed them into our rich custard cream base. Success! You'll want a few cookies with this one. May we suggest the Ginger Molasses (p. 200)?

# GINGERBREAD

MAKES ABOUT 1 QUART

1. Prepare an ice bath (p. 25).

2. In a medium-sized saucepan, combine all the ingredients except egg yolks. Stir over medium-high heat for about 5 minutes, until steam begins to rise from the surface. Remove from heat.

3. While the dairy is warming, whisk the egg yolks in a medium-sized bowl. To temper the yolks, slowly pour 1 cup of the heated cream mixture into the yolks while whisking vigorously. Continue adding heated cream and whisking until about half of the hot cream has been added. Transfer the yolk mixture to the pan.

4. Cook the mixture over medium heat, stirring continuously with a heatproof spatula, until the mixture is thick enough to coat the spatula or a digital thermometer reads 180°F (about 5-6 minutes). Immediately remove from heat and strain the custard through a fine-mesh sieve into the inner bowl of the prepared ice bath.

5. Cool the custard in the ice bath until room temperature, stirring occasionally. Cover and chill in the refrigerator for at least 4 hours, or overnight.

6. Place storage container in the freezer to chill. Freeze the mixture in an ice cream maker according to the manufacturer's instructions until ice cream is thick and creamy and has increased in volume by about a third.

7. Enjoy immediately or freeze 2 hours in chilled storage container for a firmer scoop. For storage tips see p. 28.

2 cups (473 ml) heavy cream

1 cup (236 ml) whole milk

½ cup (100 g) firmly packed dark brown sugar

2 Tbsp (35 g) fancy molasses

1 Tbsp ground cinnamon

2 tsp ground ginger

1 tsp ground cloves

¼ tsp ground nutmeg

¼ tsp fine sea salt

5 large egg yolks (90 g)

Richard Pratt is an expert on generators. Over the years, we have been incredibly lucky to have his help keeping our little fleet of ice cream trucks humming along. He also loves hot peppers. When he offered us a jar of his fiery red pepper jelly to go with ice cream, we had to try churning a hot pepper ice cream. This is the result, stamped "Richard-approved." We recommend a habanero pepper jelly for its beautiful colour and the perfect amount of chili-pow.

# HOT PEPPER

MAKES ABOUT 1 QUART

1. Prepare an ice bath (p. 25).

2. In a medium-sized saucepan, combine cream, milk, sugar, 1 table-spoon hot pepper jelly and salt. Stir over medium-high heat for about 5 minutes, until steam begins to rise from the surface. Remove from heat.

3. While the dairy is warming, whisk the egg yolks in a medium-sized bowl. To temper the yolks, slowly pour 1 cup of the heated cream mixture into the yolks while whisking vigorously. Continue adding heated cream and whisking until about half of the hot cream has been added. Transfer the yolk mixture to the pan.

4. Cook the mixture over medium heat, stirring continuously with a heatproof spatula, until the mixture is thick enough to coat the spatula or a digital thermometer reads 180°F (about 5–6 minutes). Immediately remove from heat and strain the custard through a fine-mesh sieve into the inner bowl of the prepared ice bath.

5. Cool the custard in the ice bath until room temperature, stirring occasionally. Cover and chill in the refrigerator for at least 4 hours, or overnight.

6. Place storage container in the freezer to chill. Freeze the mixture in an ice cream maker according to the manufacturer's instructions until ice cream is thick and creamy and has increased in volume by about a third.

7. Spoon a few scoops of just-churned ice cream into your storage container. Dollop some of the hot pepper jelly on top. Using a butter knife, gently swirl the jelly into the ice cream. Repeat by layering with the remaining ice cream and jelly.

8. Enjoy immediately or freeze 2 hours for a firmer scoop. For storage tips see p. 28.

2 cups (473 ml) heavy cream

1 cup (236 ml) whole milk

½ cup (100 g) sugar

2 Tbsp (50 g) hot pepper jelly, divided

¼ tsp fine sea salt

5 large egg yolks (90 g)

This is your New Year's Eve ice cream, for when the kids are tucked into bed and the adults are ringing in the new year in style. In other words, with ice cream. Best enjoyed with a glass of champagne.

# GRAPEFRUIT & ROSEMARY SPARKLER

MAKES ABOUT 1 QUART

1. Prepare an ice bath (p. 25).

2. In a medium-sized saucepan, combine cream, milk, grapefruit juice, rosemary, sugar and salt. Stir over medium-high heat for about 5 minutes, until steam begins to rise from the surface. Remove from heat. Cover and steep for 5 minutes.

3. While the dairy is warming, whisk the egg yolks in a medium-sized bowl. To temper the yolks, slowly pour 1 cup of the heated cream mixture into the yolks while whisking vigorously. Continue adding heated cream and whisking until about half of the hot cream has been added. Transfer the yolk mixture to the pan.

4. Cook the mixture over medium heat, stirring continuously with a heatproof spatula, until the mixture is thick enough to coat the spatula or a digital thermometer reads 180°F (about 5–6 minutes). Immediately remove from heat and strain the custard through a fine-mesh sieve into the inner bowl of the prepared ice bath.

5. Stir in the sparkling wine and grapefruit zest. Cool the custard in the ice bath until room temperature, stirring occasionally. Cover and chill in the refrigerator for at least 4 hours, or overnight.

6. Place storage container in the freezer to chill. Freeze the mixture in an ice cream maker according to the manufacturer's instructions until ice cream is thick and creamy and has increased in volume by about a third.

7. Enjoy immediately or freeze 2 hours in chilled storage container for a firmer scoop. For storage tips see p. 28.

2 cups (473 ml) heavy cream

1 cup (236 ml) whole milk

½ cup (118 ml) fresh pink grapefruit juice

2 sprigs rosemary

¾ cup (150 g) sugar

¼ tsp fine sea salt

5 large egg yolks (90 g)

½ cup (118 ml) sparkling white wine, such as Prosecco (see Booze tip, p. 157)

1 Tbsp grapefruit zest (about 1 grapefruit)

Cold days are always welcome for our staffer Maddy if they mean this flavour is in the lineup. It has all the hallmarks of that quintessential après-tobogganing drink, complete with mini marshmallows.

# HOT COCOA

MAKES ABOUT 1 QUART

### MINI MARSHMALLOWS

1. Tear each marshmallow into quarters and lay flat on a baking sheet or large dinner plate. Try to separate the bits as much as possible. If the marshmallows are too sticky to work with, fill a shallow bowl with warm water and dunk in your fingers before tearing. Freeze marshmallow pieces on the baking sheet until needed.

   Marshmallows can be stored in a small airtight container in the freezer for up to 1 month. Makes ½ cup.

### HOT COCOA ICE CREAM

2. Prepare an ice bath (p. 25).

3. In a medium-sized saucepan, combine cream, milk, sugar, cocoa and salt. Whisk over medium-high heat for 5 minutes, or until steam begins to rise from the surface. Remove from heat.

4. While the dairy is warming, whisk the egg yolks in a medium-sized bowl. To temper the yolks, slowly pour 1 cup of the heated cream mixture into the yolks while whisking vigorously. Continue adding heated cream and whisking until about half of the hot cream has been added. Transfer the yolk mixture to the pan.

5. Cook the mixture over medium heat, stirring continuously with a heatproof spatula, until the mixture is thick enough to coat the spatula or a digital thermometer reads 180°F (about 5–6 minutes). Immediately remove from heat and strain the custard through a fine-mesh sieve into the inner bowl of the prepared ice bath.

### MINI MARSHMALLOWS
½ cup (25 g) mini marshmallows

### HOT COCOA ICE CREAM
2 cups (473 ml) heavy cream

1 cup (236 ml) whole milk

¾ cup (150 g) sugar

2 Tbsp Dutch-processed cocoa powder

¼ tsp fine sea salt

5 large egg yolks (90 g)

1 tsp pure vanilla extract

1 qty Mini Marshmallows (see here)

6. Stir in vanilla. Cool the custard in the ice bath until room temperature, stirring occasionally. Cover and chill in the refrigerator for at least 4 hours, or overnight.

7. Place storage container in the freezer to chill. Freeze the mixture in an ice cream maker according to the manufacturer's instructions until ice cream is thick and creamy and has increased in volume by about a third.

8. Once churned, add in marshmallows and churn for a further 30 seconds until incorporated.

9. Enjoy immediately or freeze 2 hours in chilled storage container for a firmer scoop. For storage tips see p. 28.

Our dreaming-of-going-south-but-stuck-here-in-the-Canadian-winter (adult) ice cream flavour. It's a rich blend of coconut cream, Caribbean rum and sweet, tangy pineapple, best served with a glossy red cherry and a kitschy pink umbrella.

# PIÑA COLADA

VEGAN   MAKES ABOUT 1 QUART

### PINEAPPLE RUM

1. Combine pineapple, brown sugar and lemon juice in a medium-sized saucepan. Bring to a simmer over medium-high heat, then reduce heat to medium. Simmer for 4–5 minutes, until sauce is syrupy and pineapple is slightly softened. Transfer to a food processor and purée. Stir in rum. Set aside to cool.

   Pineapple rum can be stored in a sealed glass jar in the refrigerator for up to 1 week. Makes about ½ cup.

### PIÑA COLADA ICE CREAM

2. Toast coconut in a large skillet over medium-low heat for 5 minutes, stirring often, until golden brown and very fragrant. Set aside.

   Cooled coconut can be stored in an airtight container at room temperature for 1 week.

3. Prepare an ice bath (p. 25).

4. Scoop out 1½ cups (350 g) coconut cream from the chilled cans of coconut milk and reserve coconut water for another use. Whisk together coconut cream, coconut milk, sugar, pineapple juice and salt in a medium-sized saucepan. Stir over medium-high heat for 5–7 minutes, until sugar is dissolved and no visible bits of coconut cream remain. Remove from heat and strain through a fine-mesh sieve into the inner bowl of the prepared ice bath.

5. Stir in rum. Cool the ice cream base in the ice bath until room temperature, stirring occasionally. Cover and chill in the refrigerator for at least 4 hours, or overnight.

### PINEAPPLE RUM

1 cup (180 g) diced fresh pineapple

2 Tbsp (25 g) light brown sugar

1 tsp fresh lemon juice

1 Tbsp premium Caribbean white rum

### PIÑA COLADA ICE CREAM

¼ cup (21 g) shredded unsweetened coconut

2 (400 ml) cans coconut milk, chilled for 24 hours

1 (400 ml) can coconut milk, room temperature

1 cup (200 g) sugar

¼ cup (59 ml) pineapple juice

¼ tsp fine sea salt

2 Tbsp (30 ml) premium Caribbean rum

1 qty Pineapple Rum (see here)

6. Once the base is chilled, you may notice a layer of solids on the top. Give it all a quick mix to incorporate before churning. Place storage container in the freezer to chill. Freeze the mixture in an ice cream maker according to the manufacturer's instructions until ice cream is thick and creamy and has increased in volume by about a third. The base is ready when (with the machine turned off) you can scoop a big spoon of it and watch the ice cream fall back into the bowl in thick trails.

7. Once churned, add in toasted coconut and pineapple rum and churn for a further 30 seconds until incorporated.

8. Enjoy immediately or freeze 2 hours in chilled storage container for a firmer scoop. For storage tips see p. 28.

**BOOZE**

When used in moderation, alcohol, with its low freezing point, can help you achieve a quintessential parlour-style scoop. Even if you're not looking for a booze-forward flavour, 1 tablespoon of a mildly flavoured alcohol can significantly help with scoopability. Adding more than 3 or 4 tablespoons of hard alcohol can make your ice cream too soft, or it can inhibit freezing all together—so be wary and follow the recipe. Alcohol should be added to the ice cream mixture only after the saucepan has been removed from the heat, otherwise it will cook off.

Piña Colada
(p. 156)

Snow Day!
(p. 160)

An ice cream to honour our wintry Canadian childhoods—those rare and precious days when we'd wake up to the radio DJ announcing that schools were closed because of "inclement weather." We wanted to create a flavour that captured the joy of a kid facing a fun-filled, carefree weekday of tobogganing, snowball fights and fort making. So we came up with this one, a beautiful flavour for a beautiful day studded with happy-making treats.

# SNOW DAY!

MAKES ABOUT 1 QUART

### CHOCOLATE TRUFFLE BATTER

1. In a medium-sized bowl, combine chocolate, salt and espresso powder. Set aside.

2. In a small saucepan, bring cream and butter to a simmer over medium heat. Once butter is melted, pour mixture over the chocolate mixture. Set aside for 1 minute, or until chocolate chunks are significantly softened, then whisk to combine. If some stubborn chocolate chunks remain, return to the heat until the mixture is completely smooth.

3. Chill in the refrigerator for 30 minutes, or until solid.

   Batter can be stored in an airtight container in the refrigerator for up to 1 week. Makes about ¾ cup.

### SNOW DAY! ICE CREAM

4. Prepare an ice bath (p. 25).

5. In a medium-sized saucepan, combine cream, milk, sugar and salt. Stir over medium-high heat for about 5 minutes, until steam begins to rise from the surface. Remove from heat.

6. While the dairy is warming, whisk the egg yolks in a medium-sized bowl. To temper the yolks, slowly pour 1 cup of the heated cream mixture into the yolks while whisking vigorously. Continue adding heated cream and whisking until about half of the hot cream has been added. Transfer the yolk mixture to the pan.

**CHOCOLATE TRUFFLE BATTER**

½ cup (85 g) finely chopped dark chocolate (70-75% cocoa)

⅛ tsp fine sea salt

½ tsp espresso powder

¼ cup (59 ml) heavy cream

½ Tbsp (14 g) unsalted butter

**SNOW DAY! ICE CREAM**

2 cups (473 ml) heavy cream

1 cup (236 ml) whole milk

½ cup (100 g) sugar

¼ tsp fine sea salt

5 large egg yolks (90 g)

2 tsp pure vanilla extract

1 qty Chocolate Truffle Batter (see here)

¼ cup (42 g) coarsely chopped white chocolate

1 qty Raspberry Sauce (p. 196)

7.  Cook the mixture over medium heat, stirring continuously with a heatproof spatula, until the mixture is thick enough to coat the spatula or a digital thermometer reads 180°F (about 5–6 minutes). Immediately remove from heat and strain the custard through a fine-mesh sieve into the inner bowl of the prepared ice bath.

8.  Stir in vanilla. Cool the custard in the ice bath until room temperature, stirring occasionally. Cover and chill in the refrigerator for at least 4 hours, or overnight.

9.  Place storage container in the freezer to chill. Freeze the mixture in an ice cream maker according to the manufacturer's instructions until ice cream is thick and creamy and has increased in volume by about a third.

10. While the ice cream is churning, use a teaspoon to scoop out rounds of truffles. It is okay if the truffles are not perfectly round or seem large; they will break up as the ice cream gets scooped. Once ice cream is churned, drop in truffles and white chocolate. Spoon a few scoops of just-churned ice cream into your storage container. Dollop some of the raspberry sauce on top. Using a butter knife, gently swirl some of the sauce into ice cream. Repeat by layering with ice cream and sauce.

11. Enjoy immediately or freeze 2 hours for a firmer scoop. For storage tips see p. 28.

This spectacularly zingy ice cream has a yummy ginger candy jab. And if you have access to a juicer, why not add ginger juice for an extra flavour punch? And if you feel like making your own candied ginger, go for it.

# FRESH GINGER

MAKES ABOUT 1 QUART

1. In a medium-sized saucepan, combine cream, milk, sugar, salt, ginger juice (if using) and ginger. Stir over medium-high heat for about 5 minutes, until steam begins to rise from the surface. Remove from heat. Cover and steep for 1 hour.

2. Reheat the mixture over medium-high heat for 3–5 minutes, or until steam begins to rise from the surface.

3. Prepare an ice bath (p. 25).

4. While the dairy is warming, whisk the egg yolks in a medium-sized bowl. To temper the yolks, slowly pour 1 cup of the heated cream mixture into the yolks while whisking vigorously. Continue adding heated cream and whisking until about half of the hot cream has been added. Transfer the yolk mixture to the pan.

5. Cook the mixture over medium heat, stirring continuously with a heatproof spatula, until the mixture is thick enough to coat the spatula or a digital thermometer reads 180°F (about 5–6 minutes). Immediately remove from heat and strain the custard through a fine-mesh sieve into the inner bowl of the prepared ice bath.

6. Cool the custard in the ice bath until room temperature, stirring occasionally. Cover and chill in the refrigerator for at least 4 hours, or overnight.

7. Place storage container in the freezer to chill. Freeze the mixture in an ice cream maker according to the manufacturer's instructions until ice cream is thick and creamy and has increased in volume by about a third.

8. Once churned, add in candied ginger and churn for a further 30 seconds until incorporated.

9. Enjoy immediately or freeze 2 hours in chilled storage container for a firmer scoop. For storage tips see p. 28.

2 cups (473 ml) heavy cream

1 cup (236 ml) whole milk

½ cup (100 g) sugar

¼ tsp fine sea salt

1 Tbsp fresh ginger juice (optional)

1 (4-inch) piece ginger, coarsely chopped

5 large egg yolks (90 g)

⅓ cup (56 g) candied ginger, finely chopped

When Medjool dates are fresh and plump and loaded with all that excellent fibre, we make Amelia's favourite frozen "shake." She contends it's our healthiest vegan ice cream flavour, and who are we to disagree?

# DATE SHAKE

VEGAN   MAKES ABOUT 1 QUART

1. Scoop out 1½ cups (350 g) coconut cream from the chilled cans of coconut milk and reserve coconut water for another use.

2. Add dates to a food processor and blend until a sticky paste forms. Transfer to a medium-sized saucepan and add coconut cream, coconut milk, sugar and salt. Scrape seeds from the split vanilla bean into the saucepan (see Tip, p. 23), then add the scraped pod. Add cinnamon. Heat the mixture over medium-high heat for 7–8 minutes, until sugar is dissolved, no visible bits of coconut cream remain and dates are incorporated. Reduce heat to low and steep vanilla pod and cinnamon stick for 20 minutes.

3. While mixture is steeping, prepare an ice bath (p. 25).

4. After 20 minutes of steeping, remove mixture from heat and strain through a fine-mesh sieve into the inner bowl of the prepared ice bath. Add the cinnamon and vanilla pod back into the mixture to intensify the flavours. Cool the ice cream base in the ice bath until room temperature, stirring occasionally. Cover and chill in the refrigerator for at least 4 hours, or overnight.

5. Once the base is chilled, you may notice a layer of solids on the top. Remove cinnamon and vanilla pod (see Tip on p. 23 for re-using the pod). Give it all a quick mix to incorporate before churning. Place storage container in the freezer to chill. Freeze the mixture in an ice cream maker according to the manufacturer's instructions until ice cream is thick and creamy and has increased in volume by about a third. The base is ready when (with the machine turned off) you can scoop a big spoon of it and watch the ice cream fall back into the bowl in thick trails.

6. Enjoy immediately or freeze 2 hours in chilled storage container for a firmer scoop. For storage tips see p. 28.

2 (400 ml) cans coconut milk, chilled for 24 hours

8 (140 g) pitted Medjool dates

1 (400 ml) can coconut milk, room temperature

1½ cups (300 g) sugar

¼ tsp fine sea salt

1 (4-inch) vanilla bean, cut lengthwise

1 cinnamon stick, broken in half

We created this recipe for our annual Ice Cream for Breakfast Day. At first it was deemed too sweet. The buttermilk added to the base came to the rescue, taming the brown sugar. If you are aiming for a chewy oatmeal cookie chunk, bake the cookies for a few extra minutes. They may seem dry but will hydrate once added to the ice cream, creating a wonderfully chewy chunk.

# BUTTERMILK, BROWN SUGAR & SALTED OATMEAL COOKIE

GLUTEN (OPTIONAL)  MAKES ABOUT 1 QUART

1. Prepare an ice bath (p. 25).

2. In a medium-sized saucepan, combine cream, buttermilk, brown sugar, oats and salt. Stir over medium-high heat for about 5 minutes, until steam begins to rise from the surface. Remove from heat.

3. While the dairy is warming, whisk the egg yolks in a medium-sized bowl. To temper the yolks, slowly pour 1 cup of the heated cream mixture into the yolks while whisking vigorously. Continue adding heated cream and whisking until about half of the hot cream has been added. Transfer the yolk mixture to the pan.

4. Cook the mixture over medium heat, stirring continuously with a heatproof spatula, until the mixture is thick enough to coat the spatula or a digital thermometer reads 180°F (about 5–6 minutes). Immediately remove from heat and strain the custard through a fine-mesh sieve into the inner bowl of the prepared ice bath.

5. Cool the custard in the ice bath until room temperature, stirring occasionally. Cover and chill in the refrigerator for at least 4 hours, or overnight.

6. Place storage container in the freezer to chill. Freeze the mixture in an ice cream maker according to the manufacturer's instructions until ice cream is thick and creamy and has increased in volume by about a third.

7. Once churned, add in oatmeal cookie bits and churn for a further 30 seconds until incorporated.

8. Enjoy immediately, perhaps alongside the cookies themselves, or freeze 2 hours in chilled storage container for a firmer scoop. For storage tips see p. 28.

2 cups (473 ml) heavy cream

1 cup (236 ml) buttermilk (see Tip)

1 cup (200 g) firmly packed light brown sugar

½ cup (50 g) rolled oats

¼ tsp fine sea salt

5 large egg yolks (90 g)

5 (115 g) Salted Oatmeal Cookies (p. 201) without chocolate chips, chopped into ½-inch cubes

---

**HOMEMADE BUTTERMILK**

To make buttermilk, put ½ tablespoon of lemon juice in a liquid measuring cup. Pour in milk until the ½ cup measure is reached. Set aside the mixture for about 5 minutes, until curdled.

It's a Maritimes thing. When a humdinger is on the horizon, you stock up on potato chips—treats to hunker down and wait out the storm. And then calories are worked off when shovelling out. This ice cream's an ode to that effort.

# SALT & PEPPER STORM CHIPS

MAKES ABOUT 1 QUART

### CHOCOLATE-COVERED STORM CHIPS

1. Line a baking sheet with parchment paper.

2. To melt the chocolate and hold at a warm temperature, you will need to make a double boiler. Fill a medium-sized saucepan with 3 inches of water and set over medium-high heat. Rest a heatproof bowl over the pan, making sure the bottom of the bowl does not touch the water. Put chocolate and oil in the bowl.

3. Stir chocolate until it is completely melted. Reduce heat to low. Dunk a potato chip in the chocolate, then hover it over the bowl and allow any excess chocolate to drip off. Place the chip on the parchment and repeat with the remaining potato chips, until all chips are coated. Wipe the condensation off the bottom of the bowl, then scrape the remaining chocolate into a small bowl and reserve. This chip-seasoned chocolate will be added to the ice cream later.

4. Chill the chips in the refrigerator, uncovered, for 20 minutes, or until the chocolate is fully set. Break up chips into bite-sized pieces and set aside.

   Chips and reserved chocolate can be stored in separate airtight containers at room temperature for up to 3 days. Makes about 1 cup chocolate-coated chips and 2-3 tablespoons chip-seasoned chocolate.

### SALT AND PEPPER ICE CREAM

5. Prepare an ice bath (p. 25).

6. In a medium-sized saucepan, combine cream, milk, sugar, salt and pepper. Stir over medium-high heat for about 5 minutes, until steam begins to rise from the surface. Remove from heat.

### CHOCOLATE-COVERED STORM CHIPS

½ cup (85 g) chocolate chips or coarsely chopped dark chocolate (70-75% cocoa)

1½ tsp coconut oil

1½ cups (about 40 g) any flavour potato chips (or an assortment)

### SALT AND PEPPER ICE CREAM

2 cups (473 ml) heavy cream

1 cup (236 ml) whole milk

½ cup (100 g) sugar

¾ tsp fine sea salt

½ tsp freshly ground black pepper

5 large egg yolks (90 g)

1 qty Chocolate-Covered Storm Chips (see here)

7. While the dairy is warming, whisk the egg yolks in a medium-sized bowl. To temper the yolks, slowly pour 1 cup of the heated cream mixture into the yolks while whisking vigorously. Continue adding heated cream and whisking until about half of the hot cream has been added. Transfer the yolk mixture to the pan.

8. Cook the mixture over medium heat, stirring continuously with a heatproof spatula, until the mixture is thick enough to coat the spatula or a digital thermometer reads 180°F (about 5–6 minutes). Immediately remove from heat and strain the custard through a fine-mesh sieve into the inner bowl of the prepared ice bath.

9. Cool the custard in the ice bath until room temperature, stirring occasionally. Cover and chill in the refrigerator for at least 4 hours, or overnight.

10. Place storage container in the freezer to chill. Freeze the mixture in an ice cream maker according to the manufacturer's instructions until ice cream is thick and creamy and has increased in volume by about a third. While the ice cream is churning, in a small saucepan, melt reserved chip-seasoned chocolate over low heat, stirring frequently.

11. Once churned, stream a tablespoon of chocolate into the ice cream and churn until incorporated, then stream in a little more. Repeat until all the chocolate is used up. If chocolate clumps to the paddle, stop churning and scrape down before continuing. Add in chocolate-covered storm chips and churn for a further 30 seconds until incorporated.

12. Enjoy immediately or freeze 2 hours in chilled storage container for a firmer scoop. For storage tips see p. 28.

**ADD-INS**

The ideal time to add in cookies, brownies and other additions is when your ice cream is fully churned. Inclusions should be room temperature, chilled or frozen—not hot—when added to ice cream.

The only exception is when you stream melted chocolate directly into the machine. The chocolate should be heated only enough to stay fluid, and not any hotter. The coconut oil will cause the chocolate to seize as soon as it hits the semi-frozen ice cream.

"Are you soaking the raisins?" "Are you grating fresh nutmeg?" "Are you using a proper Caribbean rum?" Well, we are now, thanks to the schooling by our customer Rhonda (and the fresh nutmeg her mom brought back from St. Vincent and the Grenadines). Our rum & raisin ice cream now meets her very high standards, so much so that she asked us to make a 5-quart tub for a family gathering. Apparently it passed muster there as well.

# RUM & RAISIN

MAKES ABOUT 1 QUART

### RUM-SOAKED RAISINS

1. Combine raisins and rum in a small glass jar. Secure lid and shake to combine. Set aside for at least 4 hours, until raisins plump up.

### RUM & RAISIN ICE CREAM

2. Prepare an ice bath (p. 25).

3. In a medium-sized saucepan, combine cream, milk, sugar and salt. Stir over medium-high heat for about 5 minutes, until steam begins to rise from the surface. Remove from heat.

4. While the dairy is warming, whisk the egg yolks in a medium-sized bowl. To temper the yolks, slowly pour 1 cup of the heated cream mixture into the yolks while whisking vigorously. Continue adding heated cream and whisking until about half of the hot cream has been added. Transfer the yolk mixture to the pan.

5. Cook the mixture over medium heat, stirring continuously with a heatproof spatula, until the mixture is thick enough to coat the spatula or a digital thermometer reads 180°F (about 5–6 minutes). Immediately remove from heat and strain the custard through a fine-mesh sieve into the inner bowl of the prepared ice bath.

6. Stir in rum and nutmeg. Cool the custard in the ice bath until room temperature, stirring occasionally. Cover and chill in the refrigerator for at least 4 hours, or overnight.

7. Place storage container in the freezer to chill. Freeze the mixture in an ice cream maker according to the manufacturer's instructions until ice cream is thick and creamy and has increased in volume by about a third.

8. Once churned, add in rum-soaked raisins and any additional rum from the raisins and churn for 30 seconds until incorporated.

9. Enjoy immediately or freeze 2 hours in chilled storage container for a firmer scoop. For storage tips see p. 28.

### RUM-SOAKED RAISINS
½ cup (85 g) raisins

¼ cup (59 ml) premium Caribbean rum

### RUM & RAISIN ICE CREAM
2 cups (473 ml) heavy cream

1 cup (236 ml) whole milk

½ cup (100 g) sugar

¼ tsp fine sea salt

5 large egg yolks (90 g)

2 Tbsp (30 ml) premium Caribbean rum (see Booze tip, p. 157)

¼ tsp ground nutmeg

1 qty Rum-Soaked Raisins (see here)

Created in honour of all those bleary-eyed "6 a.m. hockey practice" parents. The ones who show up at the rink with a kid and their 40-pound hockey bag, clutching a doughnut and a Tim Hortons' coffee, extra sugar, extra cream. The classic Canadian Double Double.

# DOUBLE DOUBLE–DIPPED DOUGHNUT

GLUTEN   MAKES ABOUT 1 QUART

### DOUGHNUT BITS

1. Place doughnuts on an ungreased baking sheet and freeze for 10 minutes.

   Frozen doughnuts bits can be stored in an airtight container in the freezer for up to 1 month. Makes about ¾ cup.

### DOUBLE DOUBLE-DIPPED DOUGHNUT ICE CREAM

2. Prepare an ice bath (p. 25).

3. In a medium-sized saucepan, combine cream, milk, coffee, sugar and salt. Stir over medium-high heat for about 5 minutes, until steam begins to rise from the surface. Remove from heat.

4. While the dairy is warming, whisk the egg yolks in a medium-sized bowl. To temper the yolks, slowly pour 1 cup of the heated cream mixture into the yolks while whisking vigorously. Continue adding heated cream and whisking until about half of the hot cream has been added. Transfer the yolk mixture to the pan.

5. Cook the mixture over medium heat, stirring continuously with a heatproof spatula, until the mixture is thick enough to coat the spatula or a digital thermometer reads 180°F (about 5-6 minutes). Immediately remove from heat and strain the custard through a fine-mesh sieve into the inner bowl of the prepared ice bath.

6. Cool the custard in the ice bath, stirring occasionally. Cover and chill in the refrigerator for at least 4 hours, or overnight.

7. Place storage container in the freezer to chill. Freeze the mixture in an ice cream maker according to the manufacturer's instructions until ice cream is thick and creamy and has increased in volume by about a third.

8. Once churned, add in doughnuts and churn for a further 30 seconds until incorporated.

9. Enjoy immediately or freeze 2 hours in chilled storage container for a firmer scoop. For storage tips see p. 28.

### DOUGHNUT BITS

2 Sour Cream-Glazed Doughnuts (p. 207), broken into ½-inch pieces

### DOUBLE DOUBLE–DIPPED DOUGHNUT ICE CREAM

2 cups (473 ml) heavy cream

½ cup (118 ml) whole milk

½ cup (118 ml) dark brewed coffee, warm or chilled

¾ cup (150 g) sugar

¼ tsp fine sea salt

5 large egg yolks (90 g)

1 qty Doughnut Bits (see here)

The Merry Dairy's inaugural vegan flavour, and still our favourite. The coffee flavour is bold, the texture is remarkably creamy and the sweet crackle of chocolate is scrumptious.

# COFFEE WITH CHOCOLATE FRECKLES

VEGAN   MAKES ABOUT 1 QUART

1. Prepare an ice bath (p. 25).

2. Scoop out 1½ cups (350 g) coconut cream from the chilled cans of coconut milk and reserve coconut water for another use. Whisk the coconut cream, coconut milk, sugar, freeze-dried coffee and salt in a medium-sized saucepan. Stir over medium-high heat for 5–7 minutes, until sugar and coffee are dissolved and no visible bits of coconut cream remain. Remove from heat and strain through a fine-mesh sieve into the inner bowl of the prepared ice bath.

3. Cool the ice cream base in the ice bath until room temperature, stirring occasionally. Cover and chill in the refrigerator for at least 4 hours, or overnight.

4. Once the base is chilled, you may notice a layer of solids on the top. Give it all a quick mix to incorporate before churning. Place storage container in the freezer to chill. Freeze the mixture in an ice cream maker according to the manufacturer's instructions until ice cream is thick and creamy and has increased in volume by about a third. The base is ready when (with the machine turned off) you can scoop a big spoon of it and watch the ice cream fall back into the bowl in thick trails.

5. While ice cream is churning, make the crackle. In a small saucepan, melt chocolate and coconut oil over low heat, stirring frequently.

6. Once ice cream is churned, stream a tablespoon of chocolate into the ice cream and churn to incorporate, then stream in a little more. If chocolate clumps to the paddle, stop churning and scrape down before continuing. Repeat until all the chocolate is used up.

7. Enjoy immediately or freeze 2 hours in chilled storage container for a firmer scoop. For storage tips see p. 28.

**2 (400 ml) cans coconut milk, chilled for 24 hours**

**1 (400 ml) can coconut milk, room temperature**

**1½ cups (300 g) sugar**

**¼ cup (20 g) freeze-dried coffee**

**¼ tsp fine sea salt**

**½ cup (85 g) coarsely chopped dark chocolate (70–75% cocoa)**

**1 tsp coconut oil**

### ADD-INS

The ideal time to add in cookies, brownies and other additions is when your ice cream is fully churned. Inclusions should be room temperature, chilled or frozen—not hot—when added to ice cream.

The only exception is when you stream melted chocolate directly into the machine. The chocolate should be heated only enough to stay fluid, and not any hotter. The coconut oil will cause the chocolate to seize as soon as it hits the semi-frozen ice cream.

What to do with leftover waffles? Or with all those waffles that weren't quite handsome enough to serve? You'll not be shocked to hear we make ice cream with them. This recipe was developed after our annual Ice Cream for Breakfast Day (p. 174) left us with dozens of extra waffles, bowls of fresh berries and gallons of maple syrup. It's the ideal breakfast ice cream.

# TOASTED WAFFLE & MAPLE-BERRY COMPOTE

GLUTEN   MAKES ABOUT 1 QUART

### MAPLE-BERRY COMPOTE

1. Use a fork to mash together the berries and maple syrup in a medium-sized saucepan. Cook over medium heat for 3–5 minutes, until slightly thickened. Remove from heat and stir in vanilla. Set aside to cool.

   Compote can be stored in an airtight container in the refrigerator for up to 10 days. Makes ½ cup.

### TOASTED WAFFLE ICE CREAM

2. Prepare an ice bath (p. 25).

3. In a medium-sized saucepan, combine cream, milk, sugar, maple syrup and salt. Stir over medium-high heat for about 5 minutes, until steam begins to rise from the surface. Remove from heat.

4. While the dairy is warming, whisk the egg yolks in a medium-sized bowl. To temper the yolks, slowly pour 1 cup of the heated cream mixture into the yolks while whisking vigorously. Continue adding heated cream and whisking until about half of the hot cream has been added. Transfer the yolk mixture to the pan.

5. Cook the mixture over medium heat, stirring continuously with a heatproof spatula, until the mixture is thick enough to coat the spatula or a digital thermometer reads 180°F (about 5–6 minutes). Immediately remove from heat and strain the custard through a fine-mesh sieve into the inner bowl of the prepared ice bath.

### MAPLE-BERRY COMPOTE

½ cup (71 g) assorted fresh berries

1 Tbsp pure maple syrup

¼ tsp pure vanilla extract

### TOASTED WAFFLE ICE CREAM

2 cups (473 ml) heavy cream

1 cup (236 ml) whole milk

¼ cup (50 g) sugar

¼ cup (59 ml) pure maple syrup

¼ tsp fine sea salt

5 large egg yolks (90 g)

1 (8-inch) Waffle (p. 206), toasted, buttered and cut into ¼-inch cubes

1 qty Maple-Berry Compote (see here)

6. Cool the custard in the ice bath until room temperature, stirring occasionally. Cover and chill in the refrigerator for at least 4 hours, or overnight.

7. Place storage container in the freezer to chill. Freeze the mixture in an ice cream maker according to the manufacturer's instructions until ice cream is thick and creamy and has increased in volume by about a third.

8. Once churned, drop in waffle pieces and churn for a further 30 seconds. Spoon a few scoops of just-churned ice cream into your storage container. Dollop some of the compote on top. Using a butter knife, gently swirl the compote into the ice cream. Repeat by layering with ice cream and more compote. The remaining compote can be drizzled on top of each scoop.

9. Enjoy immediately or freeze 2 hours for a firmer scoop. For storage tips see p. 28.

# ICE CREAM FOR BREAKFAST

When a mom of six from Rochester, New York, facing another February day of snow and cold, had had enough, she declared it was "Ice Cream for Breakfast Day." Apparently, her kids thought that was pretty cool and it's been a yearly tradition ever since.

That was back in the 1960s. But the mood-boosting idea of a wintry morning devoted to ice cream slowly gathered steam such that, today, Ice Cream for Breakfast Day is marked by families around the world. Truly! There are three stipulations:

1. **Eat ice cream.**

2. **Eat it on the first Saturday in February.**

3. **Eat it on that day for breakfast.**

At The Merry Dairy, it's a magical event. Kids and their parents arrive at our shop door early in the morning in their PJs (and their parkas) to indulge in breakfast-inspired ice creams created just for the day. Some arrive on skis. Others on snowshoes. Kids are pulled in toboggans. They gather in our production kitchen to enjoy scoops on hot-griddled waffles, while the theme songs of old Saturday-morning cartoons blast out nostalgia for the parents.

And after that, spring is welcome... anytime!

Toasted Waffle & Maple-Berry Compote
(p. 172)

You know that sweet corny flavour of the milk that puddles at the bottom of the cereal bowl? That's the flavour of this vegan ice cream. The texture comes from the candied flakes of cornflake brittle, along with the candied dust that's left from smashing them. Enjoy for breakfast (see sidebar, p. 174). Or as a midnight snack.

# CORNFLAKE BRITTLE

VEGAN / GLUTEN   MAKES ABOUT 1 QUART

**CORNFLAKE BRITTLE**

1. Line a baking sheet with parchment paper.

2. In a medium-sized saucepan, gently mix together the sugar and water. Attach a candy thermometer to the pan. Make sure the tip of the thermometer is fully submerged but does not touch the bottom of the pan, to ensure an accurate reading.

3. Bring to a boil over high heat for 3½–4½ minutes. As the mixture cooks, resist the urge to stir. Gently swirl the pot if some spots are browning faster than others.

4. Meanwhile, place measured cornflakes and baking soda next to the stove. Keep an oven mitt (to protect your mixing hand from hot steam) and whisk nearby.

5. Boil until light golden and a digital thermometer reads between 350°F and 360°F. Put on the oven mitt and whisk in baking soda. The mixture will be very hot and billow up, then settle down. Add cornflakes and mix to coat. Quickly and carefully transfer the mixture to the prepared baking sheet. Set aside to cool.

6. Using your hands or a blunt kitchen utensil (like the handle of a whisk), break cornflake slab into chunks no larger than a quarter. The candy will shatter into many different sizes—and you will want it all! Using both the candy dust and the larger pieces will given the ice cream a nice textural component.

   Cornflake brittle can be stored in an airtight container at room temperature for up to 2 weeks. Makes about 2 cups.

**CORNFLAKE BRITTLE**
¾ cup (150 g) sugar
2 Tbsp (30 ml) water
1 cup (35 g) cornflakes
½ tsp baking soda

## CORNFLAKE ICE CREAM

7.  Scoop out 1½ cups (350 g) coconut cream from the chilled cans of coconut milk and reserve coconut water for another use. Whisk the coconut cream, coconut milk, sugar and salt in a medium-sized saucepan. Stir over medium-high heat for 5–7 minutes, until sugar is dissolved and no visible bits of coconut cream remain. Stir in cornflakes, then reduce heat to low and steep cereal for 20 minutes.

8.  While mixture is steeping, prepare an ice bath (p. 25).

9.  After 20 minutes of steeping, remove mixture from heat and strain through a fine-mesh sieve into the inner bowl of the prepared ice bath, pressing down on the cereal with a stiff rubber spatula to extract as much flavour as possible. Cool the ice cream base in the ice bath until room temperature, stirring occasionally. Cover and chill in the refrigerator for at least 4 hours, or overnight.

10. Once the base is chilled, you may notice a layer of solids on the top. Give it all a quick mix to incorporate before churning. Place storage container in the freezer to chill. Freeze the mixture in an ice cream maker according to the manufacturer's instructions until ice cream is thick and creamy and has increased in volume by about a third. The base is ready when (with the machine turned off) you can scoop a big spoon of it and watch the ice cream fall back into the bowl in thick trails.

11. Once churned, add in cornflake brittle and churn for a further 30 seconds until incorporated.

12. Enjoy immediately or freeze 2 hours in chilled storage container for a firmer scoop. For storage tips see p. 28.

## CORNFLAKE ICE CREAM

2 (400 ml) cans coconut milk, chilled for 24 hours

1 (400 ml) can coconut milk, room temperature

1½ cups (300 g) sugar

¼ tsp fine sea salt

2 cups (70 g) cornflakes

¼ cup (37 g) Cornflake Brittle (see here), plus extra for garnish

Brown that butter—it will make a big difference to the rich butterscotch flavour of this "Good morning" ice cream. We love the beautiful jams from Ottawa's Top Shelf Preserves for the swirls: Strawberry Rhubarb, Plum or Sour Cherry & Rose. And if you really want to play with the end colour, try their Blueberry Gin jam.

# BUTTERED TOAST & JAM

GLUTEN    MAKES ABOUT 1 QUART

### TOASTED CRUMBS

1. Preheat oven to 325°F.

2. Place bread on a baking sheet and bake for 15-20 minutes, or until bread is golden brown and very dry. Set aside to cool completely.

3. Transfer bread to a food processor and pulse to a fine crumb.

   Toasted crumbs can be stored in a small airtight container at room temperature for up to 3 days. Makes about ¼ cup.

### BUTTERED TOAST & JAM ICE CREAM

4. Prepare an ice bath (p. 25).

5. Melt butter in a medium-sized saucepan over medium heat. Cook for 3-4 minutes, stirring continuously, until butter foams, turns chestnut brown and smells nutty.

6. Add cream, milk, sugar and salt to the pan. Stir over medium-high heat for about 5 minutes, until steam begins to rise from the surface. Remove from heat. Use an immersion blender to fully incorporate any butter solids.

7. While the dairy is warming, whisk the egg yolks in a medium-sized bowl. To temper the yolks, slowly pour 1 cup of the heated cream mixture into the yolks while whisking vigorously. Continue adding heated cream and whisking until about half of the hot cream has been added. Transfer the yolk mixture to the pan.

8. Cook the mixture over medium heat, stirring continuously with a heatproof spatula, until the mixture is thick enough to coat the spatula or a digital thermometer reads 180°F (about 5-6 minutes). Immediately remove from heat and strain the custard through a fine-mesh sieve into the inner bowl of the prepared ice bath.

**TOASTED CRUMBS**
1 slice brioche bread

**BUTTERED TOAST & JAM
ICE CREAM**
2 Tbsp (28 g) unsalted butter, room temperature

2 cups (473 ml) heavy cream

1 cup (236 ml) whole milk

¾ cup (150 g) sugar

¼ tsp fine sea salt

5 large egg yolks (90 g)

1 Tbsp Toasted Crumbs (see here)

½ cup (118 g) of your favourite homemade or store-bought jam

9.  Cool the custard in the ice bath until room temperature, stirring occasionally. Cover and chill in the refrigerator for at least 4 hours, or overnight.

10. Just before freezing, check to see if the butter has solidified—if so, blitz with an immersion blender to combine. Stir in toasted crumbs. Place storage container in the freezer to chill. Freeze the mixture in an ice cream maker according to the manufacturer's instructions until ice cream is thick and creamy and has increased in volume by about a third.

11. Spoon a few scoops of just-churned ice cream into your storage container. Dollop the jam on top. Using a butter knife, gently swirl the jam into the ice cream. Repeat by layering with ice cream and more jam. Garnish with leftover toasted crumbs before serving.

12. Enjoy immediately or freeze 2 hours for a firmer scoop. For storage tips see p. 28.

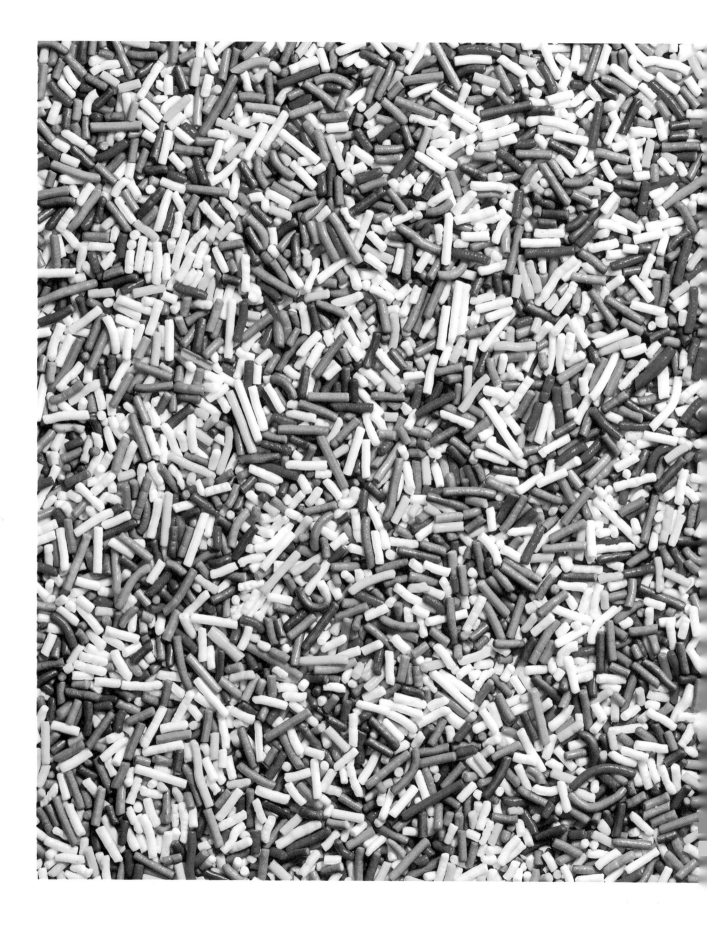

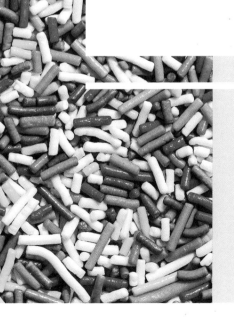

# MERRY DESSERTS

You're on dessert for the potluck? Need to shake up the Christmas feast's sweet ending? It's your nephew's tenth birthday and you're looking for some wow? Even the simple ice cream sandwich can be pyramided up to fete a birthday in style.

# ICE CREAM SANDWICH

GLUTEN    MAKES 1 ICE CREAM SANDWICH

1. Place cookies in the freezer for 10 minutes. This helps prevent them from crumbling when compressed.

2. Place a chilled cookie, face down, on your clean work surface. Put a scoop of ice cream in the centre of the cookie. The ice cream should cover only two-thirds of the cookie. Place the second cookie on top, then carefully press down so that the ice cream spreads to the perimeters of the cookies.

3. Spread topping (if using) on a plate. Roll the cookies in it edgewise so that the toppings adhere to the ice cream. Eat immediately or wrap in parchment paper and freeze for up to 1 week.

**2 favourite cookies (2 different flavours can also work!)**

**1 scoop fully frozen ice cream of your choice**

**Sprinkles, coconut or mini chocolate chips, for topping (optional)**

### ICE CREAM SANDWICH PYRAMID

Place frozen ice cream sandwiches on a cake round, then tower sandwiches up layer by layer to create a pyramid as tall as you dare. For the ultimate celebratory dessert, stud immediately after assembly with sparklers, edible glitter and/or birthday candles.

A cake with big-time wow and without the need for an oven. Doesn't get much better. This recipe provides the building blocks for making any ice cream cake. You provide the creativity. We recommend freshly churned ice cream for this cake, as it's soft enough to fill the cake pan and spread out evenly. Fully frozen ice cream can be used, but it may melt somewhat by the time it's soft enough to spread—and melting and refreezing is a huge no-no.

# ICE CREAM CAKE

GLUTEN   MAKES 1 (6-INCH) CAKE

1. Pulse cookies in a food processor to a fine crumb.

2. In a medium-sized bowl, combine cookie crumbs and chocolate sauce, mixing with your fingers. (The mixture will be very sticky!) Transfer to a 6-inch springform pan and press crust into an even layer. Freeze for 30 minutes or cover tightly with a clean tea towel and freeze for up to 2 weeks.

3. When the ice cream is fresh out of the machine, pour half of it into the crust. Using an offset spatula or the back of a spoon, smooth out the ice cream to remove any large air pockets. If desired, top with sauce, whipped cream, cookie bits or candies. Add the remaining ice cream and smooth out, again removing any large air pockets. Cover and place pan in a flat spot in the freezer and freeze overnight, or until completely frozen.

4. To pop the cake out of the pan, run a tea towel under hot water, then wring it out. Undo the pan's side latch and wrap the ring with the hot towel, rewarming the towel as necessary for the ring to be eased off.

5. Top the cake with more sauce or decorations if desired. To add a drip to the cake, use a spoon to drizzle a sauce overtop and gently nudge it over the edge. Freeze to set. Before serving, set cake aside for 10–15 minutes to soften slightly, then slice and serve.

Cake can be stored in an airtight container in the freezer for up to 2 weeks.

**10 Oreos or homemade cookies**

**¼ cup (59 ml) Chocolate Sauce (p. 198)**

**1 qty freshly churned ice cream**

**1 qty of your favourite sauce (p. 196–98), for drizzling (optional)**

**Whipped cream, candies, cookie bits or your favourite decorations (optional)**

### DOUBLE TIME

Level up this ice cream cake by adding a second flavour to the mix! At step 3, fill half the pan with your first flavour of ice cream and freeze for at least 2 hours. Then fill the remaining half with your freshly churned second flavour and freeze overnight, or until completely frozen. Continue with steps 4–5. This will yield a slightly taller cake, but who's complaining?

Ice Cream Sandwiches
(p. 182)

Ice Cream Cake (p. 183), Lemon Flapper Pie (p. 186) &
Kool-Aid Meringue Kisses (p. 199)

Our ode to the Prairies, tarted up. The classic flapper pie has a graham cracker crust, a rich custard filling and a tower of meringue. This version takes some Ontario liberties with its bold lemon flavour—and, of course, with ice cream swapping in for custard—but given how fabulous it is, we think we'll be forgiven.

# LEMON FLAPPER PIE

GLUTEN   MAKES 1 (9-INCH) ICE CREAM PIE

### GRAHAM CRUST

1. In a medium-sized bowl, combine all the ingredients. Transfer mixture to a 9-inch pie plate and press the crust evenly in the bottom and up the sides of the pie plate.

   Crust can be stored in an airtight container in the refrigerator for up to 1 week.

### LEMON ICE CREAM

2. Prepare an ice bath (p. 25).

3. In a medium-sized saucepan, combine cream, milk, sugar, lemon juice and salt. Stir over medium-high heat for about 5 minutes, until steam begins to rise from the surface. Remove from heat.

4. While the dairy is warming, whisk the egg yolks in a medium-sized bowl. To temper the yolks, slowly pour 1 cup of the heated cream mixture into the yolks while whisking vigorously. Continue adding heated cream and whisking until about half of the hot cream has been added. Transfer the yolk mixture to the pan.

5. Cook the mixture over medium heat, stirring continuously with a heatproof spatula, until the mixture is thick enough to coat the spatula or a digital thermometer reads 180°F (about 5-6 minutes). Immediately remove from heat and strain the custard through a fine-mesh sieve into the inner bowl of the prepared ice bath.

6. Stir in lemon zest. Cool the custard in the ice bath until room temperature, stirring occasionally. Cover and chill in the refrigerator for at least 4 hours, or overnight.

### GRAHAM CRUST

1½ cups (180 g) graham crumbs

6 Tbsp (84 g) butter, melted

2 Tbsp (25 g) sugar

¼ tsp fine sea salt

### LEMON ICE CREAM

2 cups (473 ml) heavy cream

½ cup (118 ml) whole milk

¾ cup (150 g) sugar

½ cup (118 ml) fresh lemon juice (3-4 lemons)

¼ tsp fine sea salt

5 large egg yolks (90 g)

2 Tbsp (12 g) lemon zest (about 2 large lemons)

7. Freeze the mixture in an ice cream maker according to the manufacturer's instructions until ice cream is thick and creamy and has increased in volume by about a third.

8. Pour the freshly churned ice cream into the graham crust and spread it evenly over the crust using an offset spatula or the back of a spoon. Place the pie in a flat spot in the freezer and freeze for 4 hours, or overnight.

### MERINGUE

9. Bring 3 inches of water to a simmer in a medium-sized saucepan. Put egg whites, sugar, cream of tartar and salt in a heatproof bowl and rest the bowl over the simmering water. Whisk ingredients together for 1–2 minutes, until frothy and sugar is dissolved. To test that the sugar is dissolved, pinch a bit of meringue and rub it between your fingers—it should not feel gritty. If the sugar is not yet dissolved, beat for another 2 minutes. Remove the bowl from the pan and wipe the condensation off the bottom.

10. Using either a hand mixer or a stand mixer fitted with the whisk attachment, whisk egg white mixture on low speed for 1 minute. (Make sure the equipment is very clean and dry, otherwise the meringue won't aerate properly.) Increase speed to high and whisk for 5 minutes, or until egg whites are glossy and have stiff peaks (see Tip, p. 199). Whisk in vanilla. Makes about 1 cup.

### ASSEMBLY

11. Tower the meringue on top of the frozen pie and use a kitchen torch to char. Freeze uncovered for at least 1 hour before serving. Remove the pie from the freezer 10 minutes before you plan to slice and serve it.

Leftovers can be stored in an airtight container in the freezer for up to 2 weeks.

**MERINGUE**

2 large egg whites (70 g), room temperature

6 Tbsp (75 g) sugar

½ tsp cream of tartar

¼ tsp fine sea salt

½ tsp pure vanilla extract

At the shop, we make ice cream–filled profiteroles and stack them high to create a festive croquembouche drizzled with caramel. If you have the right freezer to accommodate such a tower, go for it. Otherwise, you could present these profiteroles as dessert "flights" on a long, thin board, each topped with a different sauce for a dramatic display.

# ICE CREAM PROFITEROLES

GLUTEN  MAKES 18

### EGG WASH

1. Beat egg and water in a small bowl until well combined.

### PROFITEROLES

2. Trace 2-inch rounds onto 2 sheets of parchment paper, evenly spacing them 1 ½ inches apart. (A consistent size means consistent baking!) Line 2 baking sheets with the parchment, ink-side down. Fit a ½-inch plain tip into a piping bag.

3. In a medium-sized saucepan, combine water, milk, butter, sugar and salt and bring to a boil over medium-high heat. Stir in flour and reduce heat to medium-low. Mix for 1–2 minutes, until flour is completely incorporated, the dough gathers into a thick, smooth ball and a thin film forms on the sides and bottom of the pan.

4. Transfer to the bowl of a stand mixer fitted with the paddle attachment, or to a large bowl if using a hand mixer. Beat the dough on low speed for 1 minute, until somewhat cooled down. Increase speed to medium. Add 3 eggs, mixing well after each addition and scraping down the bowl and paddle as needed. The batter will be shiny and quite thick—it may look curdled at first but will smooth out as more eggs are added. Dip the paddle or a spatula into the batter and lift it out. The dough hanging off the bottom should create a *V* shape. If the dough is too stiff, beat in the remaining egg.

5. Spoon the batter into the prepared piping bag. Pipe 2-inch rounds onto the baking sheet, filling in the traced circles. Set the rounds aside to rest, uncovered, at room temperature.

### EGG WASH

1 large egg

1 Tbsp water

### PROFITEROLES

½ cup (118 ml) water

½ cup (118 ml) whole milk

¼ cup (56 g) unsalted butter, cut into ½-inch cubes

1 Tbsp sugar or vanilla sugar (see Tip)

½ tsp fine sea salt

1 cup (120 g) all-purpose flour

3–4 large eggs

1 qty Egg Wash (see here)

### VANILLA SUGAR

The mighty vanilla pod can be reused once it's scraped, as it will still impart flavour. Rinse off the cream and allow it to air-dry, then add it to a bowl of sugar.

6. Preheat oven to 400°F.

7. When the oven reaches temperature, brush the mounds with egg wash. Bake for 20-25 minutes, until deep golden brown and sound hollow when tapped. When cool enough to handle but still quite warm, pierce the bottom of each profiterole with a paring knife to release steam. Cool completely.

   Unfilled profiteroles can be stored in an airtight container at room temperature for up to 2 days.

**ASSEMBLY**

8. Using a serrated knife, carefully cut profiteroles in half horizontally. Scoop ice cream onto a bottom half, then top with a profiterole "hat." Repeat with the remaining profiteroles. Drizzle a tablespoon of sauce over each profiterole. Serve immediately.

**ASSEMBLY**

1 qty fully frozen ice cream, any flavour

1 qty of your favourite sauce

Next time you are tasked with bringing dessert to the party, this recipe has you covered. It will have everyone smacking lips and demanding seconds. It starts with a coconut crust sweetened with maple syrup and scented with vanilla that's then filled with a lime ice cream that's tart and sweet, sharp and fresh. And then there's the added bonus of the crust never getting soggy, even when frozen. Garnish with toasted coconut chips if you like.

# LIME ICE CREAM PIE

VEGAN / GLUTEN (OPTIONAL)   MAKES 1 (9-INCH) ICE CREAM PIE

## COCONUT CRUST

1. Preheat oven to 350°F.

2. Combine all the ingredients in a medium-sized bowl. Press the crust into the bottom and sides of a 9-inch pie dish. Bake for 12–15 minutes, until crust is golden. Set aside to cool completely.

   Crust can be stored in an airtight container in the freezer for up to 1 month.

## LIME ICE CREAM PIE

3. Prepare an ice bath (p. 25).

4. Scoop out 1½ cups (350 g) coconut cream from the chilled cans of coconut milk and reserve coconut water for another use. Whisk together coconut cream, coconut milk, sugar, lime juice and salt in a medium-sized saucepan. Heat the mixture over medium-high heat for 5–7 minutes, until sugar is dissolved and no visible bits of coconut cream remain. Remove from heat and strain through a fine-mesh sieve into the inner bowl of the prepared ice bath.

5. Stir in the lime zest. Cool the ice cream base in the ice bath until room temperature, stirring occasionally. Cover and chill in the refrigerator for at least 4 hours, or overnight.

6. Once the base is chilled, you may notice a layer of solids on the top. Give it all a quick mix to incorporate before churning. Freeze the mixture in an ice cream maker according to the manufacturer's instructions until ice cream is thick and creamy and has increased in volume by about a third. The base is ready when (with the machine turned off) you can scoop a big spoon of it and watch the ice cream fall back into the bowl in thick trails.

### COCONUT CRUST

1½ cups (126 g) shredded unsweetened coconut

¼ cup (30 g) all-purpose flour or gluten-free flour blend

½ cup (118 ml) pure maple syrup

1 tsp pure vanilla extract

¼ tsp fine sea salt

### LIME ICE CREAM PIE

2 (400 ml) cans coconut milk, chilled for 24 hours

1 (400 ml) can coconut milk, room temperature

1½ cups (300 g) sugar

¼ cup (59 ml) fresh lime juice (about 2 large limes)

¼ tsp fine sea salt

¼ cup (24 g) lime zest (about 5 large limes)

7. Pour ice cream into the cooled coconut crust and spread it evenly over the crust using an offset spatula or the back of a spoon. Place the pie in a flat spot in the freezer and freeze overnight, or until completely frozen.

   Pie can be stored in an airtight container in the freezer for up to 2 weeks.

**ASSEMBLY**

8. When ready to serve, decorate with sliced or candied lime, zest, and toasted coconut chips. Set aside for 10 minutes to soften slightly, then slice and serve.

**ASSEMBLY**

**Lime slices or candied limes**

**Lime zest**

**Toasted coconut chips**

Lime Ice Cream Pie
(p. 190)

Yule Log
(p. 194)

It's not your traditional bûche de Noël, but we guarantee a crowd-pleaser. Go wild with the flavour combos: Merry Eggnog (p. 144) or Rum & Raisin (p. 168); a double batch of vegan Peppermint Crackle (p. 148) with Mexican Dark Chocolate (p. 109); Gingerbread ice cream (p. 151) with Salted Caramel (p. 139) or just chocolate, chocolate and more chocolate (p. 147). 'Tis the season, after all . . .

# YULE LOG

GLUTEN (OPTIONAL) MAKES 1 (10-INCH) YULE LOG (SERVES 8)

1. Silicone yule log moulds are available in many sizes. At The Merry Dairy, we use 10- × 3½-inch moulds. If you plan on using a mould larger than ours, you just need to add more ice cream (a great excuse to try out two different flavours)! If your mould is smaller than ours, simply fill the mould full, then any leftover ice cream can be transferred to a small container and stored in the freezer. You can also use metal or plastic moulds.

2. Cut brownie into a rectangle 1 inch smaller than the base dimensions of your yule log mould. For example, if the mould is 10 × 3½ inches, cut the brownie to 9 × 2½ inches. It is okay to cut a few pieces of brownie to achieve the size you need.

3. *For a one-flavour yule log:* Transfer the freshly churned ice cream from the machine to the mould. Using an offset spatula or the back of a spoon, smooth out ice cream to remove any large air pockets. Place brownie on ice cream and press down until the brownie top is flush with the ice cream. Use the back of the spoon to smooth out the ice cream surrounding the brownie. This will be the bottom of your yule log, so it doesn't have to be pretty. Place log in a flat spot in the freezer and freeze for at least 4 hours or overnight, until completely frozen.

1 qty Brown-Butter Brownie (p. 203), chilled

1–2 qty freshly churned ice cream or a combination

¼ cup (25 g) Dutch-processed cocoa powder

Fresh mint leaves and candied cranberries rolled in sugar, for decoration

4. *For a two-flavour yule log:* Fill log mould a third of the way up with freshly churned ice cream, then smooth it out with an offset spatula or the back of a spoon to remove any large air pockets. Place brownie on the ice cream and press down so the brownie is slightly submerged. Freeze for at least 4 hours. Layer the fresh churned second flavour into the mould. Fill until ice cream is in line with the top of the mould. Using an offset spatula or the back of a spoon, smooth out ice cream, again removing any large air pockets. Place the log in a flat spot in the freezer and freeze for at least 4 hours or overnight, until completely frozen.

5. Place ice cream on a serving tray, ice cream side down. Peel off the mould to reveal the ice cream yule log. (If you are using a metal or plastic mould, a hot cloth can be wrapped around the mould to soften the ice cream enough so it can be removed.)

6. Sift cocoa directly over the log. The cocoa adheres to the ice cream if it has softened ever so slightly. Decorate with mint leaves and cranberries to replicate boughs of holly. Set aside for 10–15 minutes, then slice and serve.

# SAUCES AND TOPPINGS

Here's where you can customize your ice cream based on whim and fancy and the season. What you choose to swirl through your ice cream, pair with it, dollop on top or gild it with is entirely up to you.

## STRAWBERRY SAUCE

Using fresh berries at the peak of strawberry season really makes for a bright, strawberry sauce. The sugar helps preserve it—you could freeze it and bring it out, like freezer jam, whenever you want to make a sundae during the year.

1. Combine all the ingredients in a medium-sized saucepan and cook over medium heat for 10–12 minutes, until syrupy. Remove from heat. (If desired, purée for a smooth sauce.) Set aside to cool.

   Sauce can be stored in a sealed glass jar in the refrigerator for up to 1 week or in the freezer for up to 2 months. Makes about 1 cup.

VEGAN

8-12 strawberries (200 g), thickly sliced

¾ cup (150 g) sugar

2 Tbsp (30 ml) fresh lemon juice (about 1 lemon)

## RASPBERRY OR BLACKBERRY SAUCE

This trusted sauce takes advantage of Ontario's summer bounties. We've added lemon juice to brighten the berry flavour, and we strain the seeds for a beautifully smooth sauce that ensures nothing gets stuck in your teeth!

1. In a small saucepan, combine all the ingredients except vanilla and bring to a boil over medium-high heat. Boil for 5–6 minutes, stirring frequently, until berries have broken down and sauce has thickened. Remove from heat, then stir in vanilla.

VEGAN

1 cup (112 g) fresh raspberries or blackberries

3 Tbsp (37 g) sugar

1 Tbsp fresh lemon juice (about ½ a lemon)

1 Tbsp water

½ tsp cornstarch

⅛ tsp fine sea salt

½ tsp pure vanilla extract

2. Place a fine-mesh sieve over a medium-sized bowl and push the warm sauce through the sieve to strain out the seeds. The thinner part of the sauce will go through easily (and slowly), but the pulpy bits will need to be pushed through with a flexible spatula. Discard the seeds.

Sauce can be stored in a sealed glass jar in the refrigerator for up to 1 week or in the freezer for up to 2 months. Makes about ¼ cup.

## PLUM COMPOTE

**Best made at the peak of plum season, this lovely compote is sweetened with honey and bright with lemon. Serve warm or cold on waffles, yogurt, granola or... ice cream.**

5 ripe red plums, pitted and chopped into 1-inch chunks

¼ tsp fine sea salt

2 Tbsp (30 ml) pure local honey

1 Tbsp fresh lemon juice (about ½ a lemon)

1 Tbsp water

½ tsp pure vanilla extract

1. In a medium-sized saucepan, combine all the ingredients except vanilla and bring to a boil over high heat, then reduce heat to low. Simmer for 20–25 minutes, stirring often, until plums have broken down and compote looks like a loose jam. Stir in vanilla. Set aside to cool.

Compote can be stored in a sealed glass jar in the refrigerator for up to 2 weeks. Makes about 1½ cups.

## LEMON CURD

**Nothing elevates our Damn Good Vanilla (p. 38) like a dollop of this classic curd. Or add lemon curd and graham crumbs to a cheesecake base (p. 48) for a showy dessert.**

2 large egg yolks (36 g)

½ cup (100 g) sugar

¼ cup (59 ml) fresh lemon juice (about 2 lemons)

3 Tbsp (42 g) unsalted butter, room temperature

1 Tbsp lemon zest (about 1 lemon)

¼ tsp fine sea salt

1. In a medium-sized saucepan, whisk together egg yolks and sugar. Add lemon juice, butter, lemon zest and salt. Stir over medium heat for 3–4 minutes, until butter is fully melted and curd thickens enough to coat the back of a spoon.

2. Strain curd through a fine-mesh sieve.

Curd can be stored in a sealed glass jar in the refrigerator for up to 2 weeks. Makes about ½ cup.

# CHOCOLATE SAUCE

**A classic. Using corn syrup instead of butter makes it vegan, and it keeps for ages. We highly recommend always having a jar on hand.**

1. Whisk together water, sugar and corn syrup in a medium-sized saucepan. Sift cocoa directly into the pan and whisk. Bring to a boil over medium-high heat, then immediately remove the pan from the heat. Set aside to cool, whisking periodically.

   Sauce can be stored in a sealed glass jar at room temperature for up 10 days. Makes about ½ cup.

VEGAN

¼ cup (59 ml) water

¼ cup (50 g) sugar

¼ cup (59 ml) light or golden corn syrup

6 Tbsp (37 g) Dutch-processed cocoa powder

# SALTED CARAMEL SAUCE

**Not a sauce to walk away from when the phone rings: caramelizing sugar requires full-on stove-top attention. But the results are worth it. This is one very fine sauce. Serve in and on ice cream, of course, but it's also marvellous on brownies, apple pies, chocolate mousse, pound cake, clotted cream . . . or heaped on a spoon for direct to mouth.**

1. Combine sugar and water in a heavy-bottomed saucepan. Attach a candy thermometer to the pan. Make sure the tip of the thermometer is fully submerged but does not touch the bottom of the pan, to ensure an accurate reading. Bring the mixture to a boil. As it cooks, resist the urge to stir. Gently swirl the pot to ensure even browning.

2. Meanwhile, warm cream in a small saucepan until very warm. Place measured butter next to the stove. Keep an oven mitt (to protect your mixing hand from hot steam) and whisk nearby. Once sugar has turned deep amber in colour (about 10–15 minutes), and the thermometer reads between 375°F and 380°F, remove from heat. Don an oven mitt and then add butter carefully and from a low height, whisking vigorously. The mixture will bubble up, then settle down.

3. Stream in warm cream and whisk until the bubbling has subsided. If there are clumps of caramel, cook on low heat until the clumps have dissolved. Stir in salt and vanilla. (To clean pan, see Hardened Sugar tip on p. 139.)

   Sauce can be stored in a sealed glass jar at room temperature for up to 1 week or in the refrigerator for up to 1 month. Makes about 1½ cups.

1½ cups (300 g) sugar

½ cup (118 ml) water

1 cup (236 ml) heavy cream

2 Tbsp (28 g) unsalted butter, room temperature

¾ tsp fine sea salt

1 tsp pure vanilla extract

### EXTRA SAUCY

For more inspiration, choose from these additional scoop toppers and swirlers:

Apple Pie Compote (p. 118)

Coconut Dulce de Leche (p. 132)

Maple-Berry Compote (p. 172)

Marshmallow Fluff (p. 46)

Peach Sauce (p. 92)

Roasted Rhubarb Purée (p. 57)

Sour Cherry Compote (p. 102)

Whiskey Caramel (p. 140)

Wild Blueberry Lemon Sauce (p. 78)

# THE BAKERY

Ice cream and baking go hand in hand, so it made complete sense to include a section of our favourite baked goods. Here you'll find a delicious array of sweet treats, from cookies and brownies to butter tarts and chewy meringue kisses.

## KOOL-AID MERINGUE KISSES

**Meringue kisses tend to be sickly sweet, but the Kool-Aid powder gives them a sour-candy flavour. Plus, they're just so darn pretty and cute. Dip the kisses in chocolate if you want more wow.**

5 large egg whites (200 g), room temperature

½ tsp cream of tartar

1 cup (200 g) sugar

1½ tsp any flavour Kool-Aid powder

1. Preheat oven to 225°F. Line 2 baking sheets with parchment paper.

2. Make sure the bowl of your stand mixer and whisk attachment are very clean and dry, otherwise the meringue won't aerate properly.

3. Whisk egg whites on medium speed for 1 minute, or until foamy. Add cream of tartar and increase speed to high. Add sugar, a tablespoon at a time, while the machine is running. Wait about 10 seconds between each sugar addition.

4. Beat for 8–10 minutes on high speed, until the mixture is glossy, thick and holds a stiff peak (see Tip). To test that the sugar is dissolved, pinch a bit of meringue and rub it between your fingers—it should not feel gritty. If the sugar is not yet dissolved, beat for another 2 minutes.

5. Fold in Kool-Aid powder with a rubber spatula. If you are making 1 flavour, add all the powder; if you're using multiple flavours, divide meringue equally between 3 bowls (about 110 g of meringue in each) and add ½ teaspoon of powder to each.

6. Fit a ½-inch round piping tip into a piping bag. Transfer meringue to the bag.

7. To pipe kisses, hold the bag directly over the baking sheet, squeeze and gradually pull up. Stop squeezing and then lift the piping bag away, leaving a nice pointed top. The meringue won't spread, so you can pipe the kisses very close to one another.

### PEAK PERFORMANCE

You'll have created stiff peaks when you flip the whisk so the wire loops point upward and the egg whites on the whisk are firm enough to stand straight up (a slight flop of the tip is okay). They should look like little mountains.

Other than meringue, uses for egg whites include royal icing, cocktails, angel food cake, marshmallow fluff (p. 46) and waffles (p. 206). Egg whites can be frozen for many months.

8. Bake for 1 hour, then turn off the oven and leave meringues in the oven for another 1–2 hours. (Resist any urge to open the oven door! Meringue can crack when exposed to a temperature change.) Cool completely

Kisses can be stored in an airtight container at room temperature for up to 1 week or in the freezer for up to 2 months. Makes about 100 kisses.

# GINGER MOLASSES COOKIES

**The molasses in this recipe keeps the cookies soft, making them perfect for ice cream sandwiches. It's fabulous with Salted Caramel (p. 139), Damn Good Vanilla (p. 38), Pumpkin Spice (p. 108) and Gingerbread (p. 151), of course.**

3/4 cup (170 g) unsalted butter, room temperature

1/2 cup (100 g) sugar

1/2 cup (100 g) firmly packed dark brown sugar

1/4 cup (59 ml) fancy molasses

1 large egg, room temperature

1/2 tsp pure vanilla extract

2 1/4 cups (270 g) all-purpose flour

1 1/2 tsp baking soda

1 1/2 tsp ground ginger

1 tsp ground cinnamon

1/2 tsp ground cloves

1/4 tsp fine sea salt

1/4 tsp freshly ground black pepper

1. Using either a hand mixer or a stand mixer fitted with the paddle attachment, cream butter and both sugars for 3 minutes on high speed, or until fully combined and whipped. Scrape down the sides of the bowl and paddle as needed.

2. Add molasses, egg and vanilla. Beat on high speed for 2–3 minutes, scraping down as needed, until no visible chunks of butter remain and the batter is pale. The batter may look soupy at first, but keep on beating!

3. In a separate medium-sized bowl, whisk together flour, baking soda, ginger, cinnamon, cloves, salt and pepper. Gradually add flour mixture to the butter mixture. Mix on low speed until no streaks of flour remain.

4. Cover dough with a clean tea towel, then chill in the refrigerator for at least 30 minutes or up to 24 hours.

5. Preheat your oven to 350°F. Line 2 baking sheets with parchment paper.

6. Using a #40 scoop or a spoon, place mounds of cookie dough on the prepared baking sheet, evenly spacing them 2 inches apart. Dough mounds should measure approximately 1 1/2 tablespoons.

7. Bake for 7 minutes. Remove a baking sheet from the oven, hold it about 3 inches above a tea towel placed on the countertop and then drop the sheet. This will flatten the cookies and give them crackly tops. Repeat with the second baking sheet. Return both baking sheets to the oven, rotating their positions on the oven racks. Bake for 3–5 more minutes, until the cookie edges are firm.

The centres will look slightly underdone—this is okay! Set aside for 5 minutes, then transfer to a wire rack to cool completely.

Cookies can be stored in an airtight container at room temperature for up to 1 week or in the freezer for up to 2 months. Makes 24 cookies.

## SALTED OATMEAL CHOCOLATE CHIP COOKIES

**A wonderful, all-purpose recipe with a bit of espresso to enhance the chocolate flavour, a sprinkle of finishing salt for some crunchy texture and extra chocolate chip toppers to really take things up a notch.**

1.  Using either a hand mixer or a stand mixer fitted with the paddle attachment, cream butter and both sugars on high speed for 2–3 minutes, until pale and fluffy. Scrape down the sides of the bowl and paddle as needed. Add egg and vanilla and beat on high speed for 2 minutes. Scrape down the sides again.

2.  In a separate medium-sized bowl, whisk together flour, oats, cornstarch, baking soda, salt and espresso powder (if using). With the mixer on low speed, gradually add the flour-oat mixture to the butter mixture. When flour is almost fully incorporated, add chocolate chips and mix well to disperse and so there are no streaks of flour or oats.

3.  Cover dough with a clean dish towel, then chill in the refrigerator for at least 30 minutes or up to 24 hours.

4.  Preheat oven to 350°F. Line 2 baking sheets with parchment paper.

5.  Using a #40 scoop or a spoon, place mounds of cookie dough on the prepared baking sheet, evenly spacing them 2 inches apart. Dough mounds should measure approximately 1½ tablespoons. Dot a few chocolate chips on each cookie, gently pressing the chips into the surface. Lightly sprinkle the centre of each cookie with flaky salt.

6.  Bake, rotating halfway through, for 10–12 minutes, or until the edges are lightly browned. The centres will look slightly underdone—this is okay! Set aside for 5 minutes, then transfer to a wire rack to cool completely.

Cookies can be stored in an airtight container at room temperature for up to 1 week or in the freezer for up to 2 months. Makes 20 cookies.

GLUTEN (OPTIONAL)

½ cup (112 g) unsalted butter, room temperature

½ cup (100 g) firmly packed light brown sugar

¼ cup (50 g) sugar

1 large egg

1½ tsp pure vanilla extract

½ cup (60 g) all-purpose flour or gluten-free flour blend

1¼ cups (125 g) old-fashioned rolled oats

½ tsp cornstarch

½ tsp baking soda

¼ tsp fine sea salt

½ tsp espresso powder (optional)

½ cup chocolate chips, plus extra for garnish

Flaky sea salt, for garnish

# LEMON BISCOTTI

We toss chunks of these into our Limoncello Blackberry Biscotti ice cream (p. 65). You can also add dried fruit, swap in pure almond extract for the lemon and/or replace 3 tablespoons of flour with 3 tablespoons of cocoa powder.

1. Preheat oven to 300°F. Spray a 9- × 5-inch loaf pan with cooking spray and then line with parchment paper, leaving a 2-inch overhang.

2. Sift flour, baking powder and salt into a medium-sized mixing bowl. Whisk, then set aside.

3. Using either a hand mixer or a stand mixer fitted with the paddle attachment, cream butter and sugar on high speed for 2–3 minutes, until pale and fluffy. Scrape down the sides of the bowl and paddle as needed. Add eggs, vanilla, lemon zest and lemon juice and beat on high speed for 1 minute, scraping down as needed. The mixture may look slightly curdled from the acidic lemon juice—this is okay!

4. Gradually add the flour mixture to the butter mixture and mix on low speed until just combined. Transfer mixture to the prepared loaf pan, wet your fingers, then press down on the sticky dough to pack it into the pan. Bake for 50–60 minutes, until the edges turn golden brown. Set aside for 20 minutes to cool. Leave the oven on.

5. Using the parchment overhang, lift up the loaf and transfer to a cutting board. With a serrated knife, cut into 12 slices, ½ inch wide.

6. Line a baking sheet with parchment paper. Transfer the sliced loaf to the prepared baking sheet, ensuring that there is enough space between slices for air to circulate, and bake for another 25–30 minutes, until very dry and edges are golden. Set aside to cool completely.

   Biscotti can be stored in an airtight container at room temperature for up to 2 weeks. (Storing them in a tin helps keep them crisp.) Makes 12 biscotti.

GLUTEN

Cooking spray

2 cups (240 g) all-purpose flour

1 tsp baking powder

¾ tsp fine sea salt

½ cup (113 g) unsalted butter, room temperature

¾ cup (150 g) sugar

2 large eggs

1 tsp pure vanilla extract

1 Tbsp lemon zest (about 1 lemon)

2 Tbsp (30 ml) fresh lemon juice (about 1 lemon)

# BROWN-BUTTER BROWNIES

Here's a stellar brownie recipe elevated with browned butter, espresso and a doubling of chocolate. As with all things chocolate, the better the quality of cocoa, the better the brownie.

1. Preheat oven to 350°F. Spray a 9-inch square baking pan with cooking spray and line with parchment paper, leaving a 2-inch overhang.

2. In a medium-sized bowl, sift flour, espresso powder, baking powder and salt. Whisk together, then set aside.

3. Melt butter in a medium-sized saucepan over medium heat. Cook for 5–7 minutes, stirring continuously, until butter foams, turns chestnut brown and smells nutty. Remove from heat.

4. Whisk sugar into the melted butter, then return butter to the warm (but turned off) element to keep the mixture somewhat fluid.

5. Using either a hand mixer or a stand mixer fitted with the whisk attachment, mix eggs, cocoa and vanilla on low speed for 30 seconds, then increase to medium-high speed for 1–2 minutes, until the mixture is glossy. Reduce the speed to medium-low and stream in melted butter and sugar mixture. Increase the speed to medium and whisk for 1 minute, or until fully combined. Scrape down the sides of the bowl once to incorporate.

6. Add dry ingredients to the mixer and mix on low speed until just combined. Stir in chocolate chips and mix until just combined. Pour batter into the prepared baking pan and spread evenly using an offset spatula or spoon. Bake for 25–28 minutes, until the edges start to pull away from the sides, small cracks form on the surface and the centre is just set. Set aside to cool completely.

Brownies can be stored in an airtight container at room temperature for up to 1 week. Makes 16 squares.

Note: Chilling the brownies before slicing helps achieve clean cuts.

GLUTEN (OPTIONAL)

Cooking spray

¾ cup (90 g) all-purpose flour or gluten-free flour blend

½ tsp espresso powder

½ tsp baking powder

½ tsp fine sea salt

1 cup (227 g) unsalted butter, room temperature

1½ cups (300 g) sugar

3 large eggs, room temperature

¾ cup (75 g) Dutch-processed cocoa powder

1 Tbsp pure vanilla extract

1 cup (200 g) chocolate chips

# PIE DOUGH

**To make the pie dough vegan, substitute vegetable shortening for the butter.**

1. Whisk together flour and salt in a large bowl. Add butter and toss, then separate the cubes as much as possible. Using your finger-tips, squish butter cubes into rough sheets and slightly break apart. Coat exposed butter with flour and work in butter, until the largest pieces are about ½ inch. If butter becomes glossy or squishes with little resistance, refrigerate it for 10 minutes. You don't want melted butter!

2. Create a well in the mixture and add in most of ice water, reserving a couple of tablespoons. Distribute water by picking up sections of the dough and letting it fall between your fingers. Toss, until water has been absorbed and dough is shaggy. Add the remaining water, 1 tablespoon at a time, tossing in between each addition. Knead dough 2 or 3 times, until it comes together in a uniform mass. If needed, add 1 more tablespoon of ice water—though the dough should feel dry to the touch, not tacky. The goal is to use as little liquid as possible to bind the dough.

3. Form dough into 2 disks and wrap tightly in plastic wrap. Chill in the refrigerator for at least 30 minutes and up to 3 days.

   Dough can also be stored, tightly wrapped in plastic wrap, in an airtight container in the freezer for up to 2 months. Thaw in the refrigerator overnight before using. Makes enough dough for 1 double-crust pie.

<u>GLUTEN / VEGAN (OPTIONAL)</u>

2 ½ cups (300 g) all-purpose flour

½ tsp fine sea salt

1 cup (227 g) cold unsalted butter, cut into ½-inch cubes

½ cup (118 ml) ice water

---

# BUTTER TARTS

**Of course, you may enjoy these on their own, warm from the oven, with a cup of tea. You can even add in raisins, if you must. But better yet, toss them into our Butter Tart ice cream (p. 67), for a delicious treat.**

1. Preheat oven to 425°F.

2. In a large 4-cup measuring cup with a pour spout or a medium-sized bowl, whisk together butter, maple syrup, brown sugar, vanilla, salt, eggs and cream. Set aside at room temperature until needed.

<u>GLUTEN</u>

1 cup (227 g) unsalted butter, melted and cooled slightly

¾ cup (177 ml) pure maple syrup

1 cup (200 g) firmly packed light brown sugar

1 tsp pure vanilla extract

½ tsp fine sea salt

2 large eggs

2 Tbsp (30 ml) heavy cream

1 qty Pie Dough (p. 204)

All-purpose flour, for dusting

3. On a lightly floured surface, roll out a disk of pie dough, keeping the other disk chilled in the refrigerator until needed. Roll out ¼ inch thick. Flip dough occasionally, adding more flour, as needed, to keep the dough from sticking to the work surface. Using a 4- or 5-inch cookie cutter, cut circles out of the pastry and fit them into an ungreased muffin pan. Repeat with the remaining dough. Gather the dough scraps into a ball and roll out once more for more pastry shells.

4. Thoroughly whisk the filling, then fill each tart three-quarters full. Do not overfill them or they will bubble over. Bake for 25 minutes, or until pastry is deep golden brown. Set the pans aside for 10 minutes, then use a blunt knife to pop out the tarts. Set aside to cool completely on a wire rack.

   Tarts can be stored in an airtight container at room temperature for up to 3 days or in the refrigerator for up to 5 days. Serve at room temperature. Makes 18 butter tarts.

# FROSTED BERRY TOASTER TARTS

**With their flaky crust, saucy filling and lemony frosting, these tarts are seriously delicious. We add house sprinkles for the final sparkle.**

1. Line 2 baking sheets with parchment paper.

2. To make the pastry bottom, take out 1 disk of the chilled pie dough from the refrigerator. (Keep the other disk chilling in the refrigerator.) Roll out dough on a lightly floured work surface into a rough rectangle slightly bigger than 12 × 10 inches. Pick up and rotate dough often to prevent it from sticking. Dust the surface with more flour as needed. The dough should be ⅛ inch thick. Pull out a measuring tape or ruler (it makes all the difference!) and, using a sharp knife, trim the dough into a rectangle exactly 12 × 10 inches. Rotate dough so the longer edge is facing you.

3. Slice dough in half lengthwise. Then make three cuts widthwise so you have 8 equal-sized rectangles in total. Each rectangle should be 5 × 3 inches. These will be the toaster tart bottoms. Gently transfer the bottoms to a prepared baking sheet. Chill in the refrigerator until needed.

4. Repeat with the second pastry disk, to create the toasted tart tops. Lay the tops on the second baking sheet and refrigerate for at least 20 minutes.

GLUTEN

1 qty Pie Dough (p. 204)

All-purpose flour, for dusting

1 large egg

1 Tbsp water

½ cup preferred berry sauce (p. 196)

5. Combine egg and water in a small bowl, beating with a fork to mix well.

6. Remove toaster tart bottoms from the refrigerator and brush the top of each with egg wash—this helps keep the tart together while baking. Dollop 2 teaspoons of berry filling on each tart and, using an offset spatula, lightly spread it out, leaving a ¼-inch border around the edges.

7. Take the toaster tart tops out of the refrigerator and place a top over each tart bottom and its filling. Using a fork, crimp the edges to strengthen the seal. If the dough sticks to the fork prongs, simply dip the fork in flour. Using a toothpick, prick 12 holes in the top of each tart, so steam can escape. Cover with a clean tea towel, then chill for 20 minutes and up to 1 hour.

8. Preheat oven to 375°F.

9. Brush toaster tarts with more egg wash. Bake for 20–25 minutes, until golden brown and flaky. Set aside to cool for 5 minutes, then transfer to a wire rack to cool completely.

**FROSTING**

10. Sift icing sugar into a medium-sized bowl. Mix in cream, lemon juice, vanilla and salt. The frosting will be thick.

11. Spread frosting on cooled toaster tarts with an offset spatula or butter knife, then garnish with sprinkles (if using).

Toaster tarts can be stored in an airtight container at room temperature for up to 3 days. To reheat, bake in a 350°F oven for 10 minutes. Makes 8 tarts.

**FROSTING**

1 cup (113 g) icing sugar

2 Tbsp (30 ml) heavy cream

½ tsp fresh lemon juice

½ tsp pure vanilla extract

⅛ tsp fine sea salt

Sprinkles, for garnish (optional)

# "ICE CREAM FOR BREAKFAST" WAFFLES

This terrific waffle recipe is a great way to use up all those leftover egg whites. Toss leftover waffles into our Toasted Waffle & Maple-Berry Compote ice cream (p. 172) or store them in the freezer in an airtight container for up to 2 months.

1. Preheat the waffle iron.

2. In a large bowl, whisk together flour, brown sugar, baking powder, baking soda, salt and nutmeg. Set aside.

3. In a medium-sized bowl or 4-cup measuring pitcher, whisk buttermilk, butter and vanilla. Set aside.

**GLUTEN**

1¾ cups (210 g) all-purpose flour

¼ cup (50 g) firmly packed light brown sugar

2 tsp baking powder

1 tsp baking soda

1 tsp fine sea salt

¼ tsp ground nutmeg

1¾ cups (414 ml) buttermilk (see Tip p. 164)

½ cup (113 g) unsalted butter, melted and cooled to room temperature

2 tsp pure vanilla extract

2 large egg whites (70 g)

¼ tsp cream of tartar

4. In a very clean and dry medium-sized bowl, whisk egg whites for 1 minute, or until foamy. Whisk in cream of tartar and beat for 3-4 minutes, until soft peaks form (when you flip the whisk so the wire loops point upward and egg whites are just holding a slight peak).

5. Create a well in the flour mixture, then stir in the buttermilk mixture until just combined.

6. Using a large spatula, gently mix ¼ cup of the whipped egg whites into the waffle batter. Add the remaining egg whites and fold in (see Tip).

7. Spoon ⅓-½ cup of batter onto the hot waffle iron and cook for 2-3 minutes, until waffle is golden brown. Repeat with the remaining batter.

If not eating right away, place waffles on a baking sheet and keep warm in a 200°F oven. Makes 6-8 (8-inch) round waffles.

> **FOLDING IN INGREDIENTS**
>
> Scrape a large spatula along the bottom of the bowl toward you. Scoop the mixture onto the top of the batter, and repeat until combined. Think of making a *J* motion and on the hook of the *J*, bringing the ingredients on the bottom up to the top.

# SOUR CREAM–GLAZED DOUGHNUTS

**Great on their own, or when tossed into our Double Double-Dipped Doughnut ice cream (p. 170). Like most fried things, doughnuts are best enjoyed the day (the hour!) they are made.**

**Leftovers (ha!) can be stored in an airtight container at room temperature for up to 2 days.**

### DOUGHNUTS

1. In a medium-sized bowl, sift together flour, baking powder, salt, nutmeg, and espresso powder. Whisk to combine, then set aside.

2. Using either a hand mixer or a stand mixer fitted with the paddle attachment, beat butter and sugar on medium speed for about 2 minutes, until sandy. Scrape down the sides of the bowl. Add egg yolks and vanilla and beat for 1 minute, or until paler and well combined.

3. Add the dry ingredients to the yolk mixture in three separate additions, alternating with sour cream (see Tip, p. 208). Make sure to both start and end with the flour mixture. Mix on low speed for 30 seconds, until dough forms a uniform ball. Using your hands, gently knead dough once or twice in the bowl, until everything is well incorporated. Be careful not to overwork it. Cover dough with a clean tea towel and chill in the refrigerator for 30-60 minutes.

GLUTEN

**DOUGHNUTS**

2¼ cups + 2 Tbsp (254 g) cake flour, plus extra for dusting

1½ tsp baking powder

1 tsp fine sea salt

½ tsp ground nutmeg

½ tsp espresso powder

2 Tbsp (30 g) unsalted butter, room temperature

½ cup (100 g) sugar

2 large egg yolks (36 g)

1 tsp pure vanilla extract

¾ cup (184 g) sour cream

Canola oil, for deep-frying

4. Line a baking sheet with parchment paper.

5. Turn dough out onto a lightly floured surface. Roll out ½ inch thick. Using either a doughnut cutter or 2 round cutters (3 inches for the large cut and 1 inch for the hole), cut out doughnuts. If your cutter sticks to the dough, dip it in flour, shaking off any excess before cutting. Gently reroll the scraps once, making sure not to overwork the dough, and cut out more doughnuts and holes. Any remaining scraps can then be cut into holes. Place doughnuts and holes on the prepared baking sheet, then chill in the refrigerator until needed.

6. Add oil to a heavy-bottomed saucepan to a 2-inch depth. Attach a deep-fry thermometer and heat oil over medium heat to 350°F. While oil heats up, make the glaze. Makes about 8 doughnuts and 12 holes.

**GLAZE**

7. Sift icing sugar into a medium-sized bowl. Whisk in the remaining ingredients.

**ASSEMBLY**

8. Line a plate with paper towel and place it next to the pan of oil. Carefully lower 2–3 doughnuts into oil—doughnuts will gently bubble, then float to the top. Once they float, deep-fry for 1½–2 minutes. Flip and deep-fry for another 1½–2 minutes, until golden. Using a slotted spoon, transfer doughnuts to the paper towel-lined plate. Repeat with the remaining doughnuts, working in batches to avoid overcrowding. Deep-fry holes for 2–3 minutes. Make sure to monitor the oil temperature and adjust heat as needed to maintain 350°F. Set aside to cool.

9. To set up a glaze station, place a cooling rack over the parchment-lined baking sheet (the same one used for the dough). This makes cleanup a breeze once the excess glaze has dripped off. Dunk doughnuts in glaze, then flip over to coat the other side. Place on the cooling rack and set aside for 10 minutes, or until glaze is set.

**GLAZE**

3 cups (340 g) icing sugar

½ cup (118 ml) whole milk

2 tsp fresh lemon juice

1 tsp pure vanilla extract

½ tsp fine sea salt

**ALTERNATING FLOUR & SOUR CREAM**

Adding the sour cream all at once may overwhelm the batter. By alternating the sour cream with the flour mixture, you ensure that all the fat is incorporated and the batter is not overmixed.

# WAFFLE CONES

Our fresh waffle cones keep our loyal customers returning to The Merry Dairy again and again. All you need to make them at home is an inexpensive pizzelle iron and a cone roller.

1. Preheat waffle cone iron.

2. Sift flour and salt into a medium-sized bowl. Whisk well and set aside.

3. In another medium-sized bowl, combine sugar and egg whites until fully mixed. Whisk in milk, butter and vanilla. Stir in the dry ingredients until just combined.

4. Spoon 2 tablespoons of batter onto the waffle cone iron and bake for 2–3 minutes, until golden brown.

5. Slide waffle off the iron and onto a clean work surface. The cone will be very hot but will need to be rolled immediately.

   Place the cone roller across the centre of the waffle. Fold the side closest to you over the cone roller, then roll so the edges slightly overlap. If needed, pinch the bottom of the cone to seal. Hold the cone seam side down for about 15 seconds, until mostly firm. Remove the cone from the roller and set aside to cool. Repeat with the remaining batter. Makes 10 cones.

## GLUTEN (OPTIONAL)

1 cup (120 g) all-purpose flour

¼ tsp fine sea salt

½ cup (100 g) sugar

2 large egg whites (35 g)

¼ cup (59 g) whole milk

¼ cup (56 g) unsalted butter, melted

2 tsp pure vanilla extract

### CUP PLEASE

You can also shape the hot waffle over a small bowl for 10 seconds to create a waffle cup.

### MAKE IT GLUTEN-FREE

For a delicious gluten-free option, replace the all-purpose flour with the following:

½ cup (79 g) brown rice flour

3 Tbsp (28 g) potato starch

2 Tbsp (12 g) tapioca starch

¼ tsp xanthan gum

# TROUBLE-SCOOPING

Ice cream making is not difficult! Sure, it requires a little science, a little experience, a little creativity, great ingredients and a good recipe (we have you there), but from time to time, you might encounter a result that's not quite right. Here are a few of the most common concerns, plus our suggestions for fixing something that has gone wrong—or, for things that can't be fixed, what to avoid next time.

**PROBLEM** "The coconut cream isn't separating from the coconut water in the chilled can of coconut milk."

**WHY?** You may be using an unsuitable brand (one that contains emulsifiers) or the can has not been chilled long enough.

**A SIMPLE FIX** Ensure the cans of coconut milk have chilled for at least 24 hours, and try not to jostle the can too much as you open it.

**NEXT TIME** The coconut milk you buy should contain only two ingredients: coconut and water. Full stop. We recommend always having a couple of cans of coconut milk stored in the coldest part of the refrigerator (at the bottom back), so they are thoroughly chilled and good to go whenever the craving strikes.

**PROBLEM** "My ice cream base has separated and looks curdled."

**WHY?** If you have ever soured milk to replace buttermilk, you have seen how acidic elements (like lemon juice or vinegar) can cause dairy to curdle. Acid lowers the pH of dairy.

This causes the proteins to denature, to gather and clump, resulting in a curdled appearance. This is likely to happen if too much acid has been added, if fat has been cut or if eggs have been omitted—it's fat and eggs that give the base structure.

**A SIMPLE FIX** Don't fret too much if the custard curdles slightly—it should not affect the final structure of the ice cream. So just strain, churn, chill, freeze and enjoy.

**NEXT TIME** Follow the precise ratios provided in the recipe, particularly when working with acidic elements like citrus, honey or molasses. You can also try adding the acidic ingredients after the base has been removed from the heat, strained and slightly cooled.

**PROBLEM** "My ice cream base looks like scrambled eggs."

**WHY** You've cooked the base too long or too quickly. When the yolks in a custard overcook, the proteins clump together. If not dealt with, the ice cream will have an undesirable texture and taste more like breakfast than dessert.

**A SIMPLE FIX** There is still (some) hope for a curdled base. As soon as you notice clumps forming in the base, remove the pan from the heat and strain the mixture through the fine-mesh sieve into the ice bath. If there are only a few clumps, they may be strained out. Give it a taste—if it tastes fine, proceed with chilling and churning. If it's too eggy-tasting or thin (which means you've lost the egg's emulsifying properties), you need to start again.

**NEXT TIME** Start with a good, heavy-bottomed saucepan. Once the egg yolks have been added to the dairy mixture, they need lots of attention. Continuously stir and scrape into every bend of the saucepan with a flexible heatproof spatula. Cook the base just until it's thick enough to coat the spatula's surface and such that a finger line drawn across the custard fails to fill in. The custard will continue to cook even off the heat, so transfer to your ice bath right away.

Along with stirring and scraping, using a thermometer will almost guarantee the base will not overcook. A custard thickens between 160°F and 180°F, but the end product will be creamier if the temperature is closer to 180°F. Until you gain confidence, you could cook the custard to the lower end of the temperature range.

---

**PROBLEM** "My ice cream maker is overflowing!"

**WHY?** When air is incorporated in the churning process, the overall ice cream volume increases. If the machine is overfilled, ice cream may spill over the top and will not aerate properly.

**A SIMPLE FIX** You'll have a mess to wipe up, but don't sweat it. The ice cream left in the machine will still be delicious—although, with less space for air to be incorporated (less "overrun"), it will likely produce a denser scoop.

**NEXT TIME** Only fill the ice cream machine two-thirds full. Ice cream can easily be frozen in batches. If you have a surplus of ice cream base, you can refrigerate it for up to 3 days, for churning at a later date, or freeze the unchurned base for up to 2 months. When ready to use, defrost the base in the refrigerator overnight and churn/freeze as you would a freshly made base.

---

**PROBLEM** "My ice cream won't freeze in the machine, and/or it's still gloopy even after being in the freezer for a few hours."

**WHY?** Ice cream right out of the machine will not be rock hard, nor should it be! The contents need to be soft enough for the paddle to churn. We call this stage the first freeze, as only about half of the water content has been frozen. The remaining water will solidify in the freezer, or in the second freeze. If, however, your ice cream does not freeze to a soft-serve consistency in the first freeze, then chances are the mix was too warm, the canister bowl not cold enough or the base contained too much sugar or alcohol (both of which depress freezing). If the ice cream is gloopy, gummy, tacky or sloppy after 4 hours into the second freeze, there's too much sugar or alcohol in the base.

**A SIMPLE FIX** Eat it anyway. The good news is that it will likely still taste terrific—just better served in a bowl than in a cone, or eaten straight out of the container.

**NEXT TIME** Reduce the quantity of sugar or alcohol.

---

**PROBLEM** **"My ice cream swirls have disappeared altogether."**

**WHY?** Swirls, or variegates, can add beautiful ribbons of flavour and colour to ice cream. But just as icy swirls can occur when water has not partnered with solids and the fix is to add more sugar (see "My ice cream is icy after its second freeze" problem), if too much sugar is added, the swirls can become tacky and remain mostly liquid, even when frozen. In some cases, these high-sugar swirls may disappear into the ice cream altogether. Or it's possible that you've simply overmixed the swirls such that they've become muddled.

**A SIMPLE FIX** You may be disappointed about the absent swirl, but the ice cream will still be lovely—just add a topping for colour and flavour.

**NEXT TIME** Decrease the sugar and add the swirl by hand, being careful to not overmix.

---

**PROBLEM** **"My homemade ice cream is much firmer than store-bought ice cream."**

**WHY?** Your ice cream has less air in it. The more air in an ice cream, the fluffier the ice cream is. Commercial machines spin so fast that air incorporation (called "overrun" in the biz) is, in some brands, as high as 100%. In home machines, the paddle spins more slowly, resulting in a much lower overrun, and a more luxurious-tasting product.

Commercial brands also rely on stabilizers to prolong the product's shelf life and create an ultra-scoopable product. We use egg yolks,

a natural stabilizer that reduces the formation of ice crystals and gives our scoops a rich taste and a smooth body.

**A SIMPLE FIX** At The Merry Dairy, we have a foolproof system to temper our ice cream to the perfect scooping consistency. Our tubs move from a deep freeze (-25.6°F/-32°C), to a holding temperature (-4°F/-20°C), to a tempering freezer (10.4°F/-12°C). For perfectly tempered ice cream at home, scoop a portion into a dish and let the dish rest for 5–10 minutes before eating. We understand this waiting business can be trying, but it will make a big difference to the texture and flavour of the ice cream.

**NEXT TIME** Add 1–2 tablespoons (no more) of alcohol to your ice cream base after it has been removed from the heat. This depresses the freezing temperature, resulting in a more scoopable ice cream. Vodka works well as a neutral flavour, and kirsch work well for fruit flavours. Adding an extra tablespoon of sugar, such as maple syrup, honey or molasses, also encourages softer ice cream.

---

**PROBLEM** **"My ice cream tastes flat."**

**WHY?** Did you skip the salt? Don't. It makes all the difference. Salt enhances flavour and balances other flavours. And be sure to use ripe, in-season fruit.

**A SIMPLE FIX** Flavours become muted when they are frozen, so let the ice cream soften a bit before indulging—you may find that's all that's needed. And, of course, you can always ramp up the flavour by loading on the toppings!

**NEXT TIME** Make sure you've added the salt. Use fruit that's ripe and in season. Steep flavourings, such as vanilla pod, chai spices or Earl Grey tea, for longer, and taste the chilled base before adding it to the machine. If you feel it needs a flavour-boost, add more citrus zest, a touch more vanilla extract or a tablespoon of a fruit-based liqueur.

---

**PROBLEM** "My ice cream is icy after its second freeze."

**WHY?** There are a few culprits for icy ice cream, some of which are explained in the Ice Crystals sidebar. Another is too much liquid in the base. Water makes its way into ice cream in sneaky ways—juices, coffee, tea, fresh fruit. If there is a surplus of liquid that doesn't bind with the fat and the sugar, the final product will be icy. The other culprit is not enough sugar—in a swirl, for example. The riper the fruit, the higher its concentration of natural sugars. Unripe fruit may require the addition of more sugar to prevent those nasty ice crystals.

**A SIMPLE FIX** There isn't one. The flavour will still be delicious, only the texture will be off. So eat it anyway.

**NEXT TIME** Do not reduce the fat (by opting for a lower butterfat cream) or the sugar! Follow the recipe, measure out the ingredients carefully and, remember, ice cream is meant to be a lovely, rich treat. Use ripe, in-season fruit whenever possible. For swirls opt for a good-quality store-bought jam that would have been made at the height of its fruit season.

---

**PROBLEM** "My ice cream has a greasy mouthfeel" or "There are little flecks of milk solids in my ice cream."

**WHY?** You've made butter! The ice cream was churned so long that the fat separated from the liquids, creating little buttery blobs and producing an overall greasy mouthfeel.

## ICE CRYSTALS

During the churning process, air is incorporated into the ice cream, and the first stage of freezing occurs. As part of the freezing stage, the water in ice cream is being transformed into ice crystals, essential for ice cream body and solidity. The smaller the ice crystals, the creamier the scoop. If these ice crystals get too big, they will noticeably disrupt the final texture.

The paddle of your ice cream machine works to agitate small ice crystals, moving them from the frozen canister walls to the main volume of ice cream. This constant motion allows small ice crystals to freeze independently. When ice cream takes too long to freeze, however, those small ice crystals buddy up and form larger ice crystals.

In short, the longer your machine runs, the bigger these crystals grow (recrystallize), contributing to an undesirable gritty texture.

We've said it before but it's worth repeating: make sure your ice cream base is fully chilled and the ice cream canister is fully frozen, to reduce the time your machine will run. If ice forms after the ice cream has completely frozen, the issue is likely in the thawing and refreezing. Every time the ice cream is removed from the freezer, the slight temperature drop means the small ice crystals can partner up and grow into big crystals. When the ice cream goes back into the freezer, these large crystals freeze, creating crunchy pockets of ice.

If possible, adjust your freezer to the lowest temperature and store ice cream where the temperature is coldest, in the bottom back of your freezer. And don't allow the ice cream to linger on the counter: scoop and return to the freezer immediately to prevent the dreaded thaw and refreeze cycle.

**A SIMPLE FIX** Sorry. Buttery ice cream is pretty unpleasant, though you could try adding milk, tossing in cookies and then buzzing it in a blender.

**NEXT TIME** Do not over-churn your ice cream! Make sure the ice cream base and bowl are fully chilled, to reduce the churning time.

Ice cream machines usually come with suggested timing; however, other factors, such as sugar and alcohol content, can drastically affect the freezing time. (See Churning Time, p. 28, for a list of things to look for.)

---

**PROBLEM** "My ice cream has freezer burn."

**WHY?** Ice crystals can breach your ice cream at the drop of a hat. Over time, the moisture in ice cream evaporates to the surface, and the cold air causes this moisture to freeze. These ice crystals will grow and grow until they cover the entire surface of your ice cream. This striking network of ice can compromise the ice cream's flavour, which can end up tasting stale or like "freezer air."

**A SIMPLE FIX** To redeem freezer-burnt ice cream, scrape off as much ice as you can, toss the remaining ice cream into a blender with milk and the sauce of your choice, and whirr the problem into a delicious milkshake.

## HOW TO MAKE A MILKSHAKE

In a blender, blend 2 scoops of ice cream, ½ cup of milk and 2 tablespoons of a sauce, topping, malt powder or add-in of your choice. Pour into a tall glass, load it up with whipped cream, top with a maraschino cherry and drink up.

**NEXT TIME** Freezer burn occurs when the surface of your ice cream is exposed to air. Choose a storage container that minimizes head space (the air above the ice cream and below the lid). Place a piece of parchment paper over the surface to minimize burn. Also, proper storage conditions will prolong the life of your ice cream, so store your ice cream at the bottom back of the freezer—never in the door. And lastly, scoop from the entire surface of the ice cream and avoid tunneling, so that the top remains relatively flat.

---

**PROBLEM** "I keep getting a brain freeze!"

**WHY?** You are not alone. The freeze won't last long and it won't kill you. When your mouth is overwhelmed by cold, it can trigger a sharp pain behind your forehead and temples. The cold causes arteries to constrict, then swell again, as blood rushes in to try to warm the area. This quick correction is what causes that brain-freeze sensation.

**A SIMPLE FIX** If you're particularly prone to brain freeze, try flipping the spoon upside down in your mouth so the cold ice cream touches your tongue and not the roof of your mouth. This technique also allows the flavour to land smack dab on your tastebuds.

**NEXT TIME** We know, we know, our ice creams are fabulous and it's tempting to wolf them down. But resist. The painful sensation is your brain's way of saying "Whoa there, slow down!"

# ACKNOWLEDGEMENTS

From truck to storefront to recipe book, this journey has been taken with The Merry Dairy team and the customers we love. To every team member, to every customer, thank you. You have made the last ten years a true joy.

To Anne DesBrisay, our writing partner like no other, you turned words into great stories, and even greater recipes. You are the great in *Great Scoops*.

To our Figure 1 Publishing partners—Chris, Michelle, Judy, Renate, Lara and Naomi—for understanding our vision and wowing us with the result.

To the Photolux team of Chris and Julien, Irene and Noah, who captured the essence of ice cream in stunning photo after photo.

To all who are makers and bakers, your inspiration has defined who we are. From our earliest days to today, you gave advice, shared tips and believed in this idea. That means more to us than you can even imagine. Thank you to Joanna Boyd, Gay Cook, Liz Davis, Colleen Forer, Margi Fineran, Anna Higgins, Dianne Ramdeholl, Ervin Jean-Pierre, Jodie Ostrovsky, Katie Russell, Iona Law, and especially to Holly Laham and Margaret Vant Erve.

To our science guys—Max Falkowitz, Stanley Rutledge and Dr. Stevenson—thank you for all of your molecular assistance.

And to the guinea pigs, our recipe tasters—Jill and Andy, Kate, Andy and Lori, Maddy, Ruth, Karen, Sharon, Helen and Pat, Jenna, and family members—who tested, tasted and gave honest feedback for each and every recipe.

And finally, thank you to you, our ultimate recipe taster and tester. We hope you love them all.

AMELIA  To my parents for their unwavering support, forever making my lofty goals seem attainable. To my dad, who passed along an unquenchable curiosity. To my mom, the original family baker who ignited in me a love of food. To my trio of brothers—Nick, Ben and Lucas—for teaching me the art of choosing the right hot sauce for every dish, even ice cream. To my sister-in-law, Jacqueline, a fellow dessert lover. To my grandparents for showing how food brings people together, and to never stop learning. To Marlene and Bernie, who opened me up to the whimsical world of ice cream. To my friends, for talking about all things ice cream—or anything but ice cream when that was needed too. And to Sam, my husband and closest friend, for always being by my side and nourishing my love of cookbooks. Thank you.

MARLENE  To Amelia Ryan, thank you for the idea, and everything that went along with it. To *all* my big sisters and brothers and the life we shared on the farm. To my children, Theo and Nadia—you bring both joy and inspiration. To my husband Bernie, who was the first believer and made this his life, here's to us! And finally, to my parents and Bernie's parents, whose business acumen, hard work and kindness have shaped every facet of our business, and by extension, this book.

And to all the kids and their parents whose nut or other allergies mean they have never been to an ice cream shop, please drop in next time you're in Ottawa! We would love to meet you.

# INDEX

# ABOUT THE AUTHORS

**MARLENE HALEY** (right)

Teacher-turned-businessperson Marlene Haley is the owner of The Merry Dairy, Ottawa's first ice-cream truck business dedicated to nut-free original-recipe frozen custard and premium ice cream. Since 2012, The Merry Dairy has become a favourite among locals, serving more than 100,000 signature frozen-custard cones from their shop on Fairmont Avenue and their fleet of Grumman trucks. Numerous publications and media outlets, including *Ottawa Magazine*, CBC Radio, and CTV News have chronicled the evolution of the business from a single ice cream truck to its increasing involvement in Ottawa's amazing community scene. Marlene lives in Hintonburg, Ottawa, with her husband, Bernie Etzinger, and can often be found at the shop greeting first-time customers and loyal fans.

**AMELIA RYAN** (left)

While growing up in Richmond, in the Ottawa Valley, Amelia Ryan observed how food brings family, friends and neighbours together. As she completed her major in business and communications, she reached a fork in the road ahead, where she needed to choose between a corporate life spent in front of a computer or a life of culinary creation. She chose the culinary path and hasn't looked back. As the creative director at The Merry Dairy, Amelia leads the company's effort to make beautiful ice creams by developing recipes with new flavours and formulating recipes that serve specific diets. She loves the way simple pleasures, such as a cone of ice cream, can create everlasting memories. Amelia lives in Ottawa with her husband, Sam.

**ANNE DESBRISAY**

Anne DesBrisay is an award-winning food writer, the author of *Ottawa Cooks* and three editions of *Capital Dining,* and the co-author of *Atelier* by Marc Lepine and *Coconut Lagoon* by Joe Thottungal. She was the restaurant critic for the *Ottawa Citizen* and *Ottawa Magazine* for twenty-five years, is a senior editor for *Taste & Travel* magazine and a judge for the Canadian Culinary Championships. She lives in Ottawa.

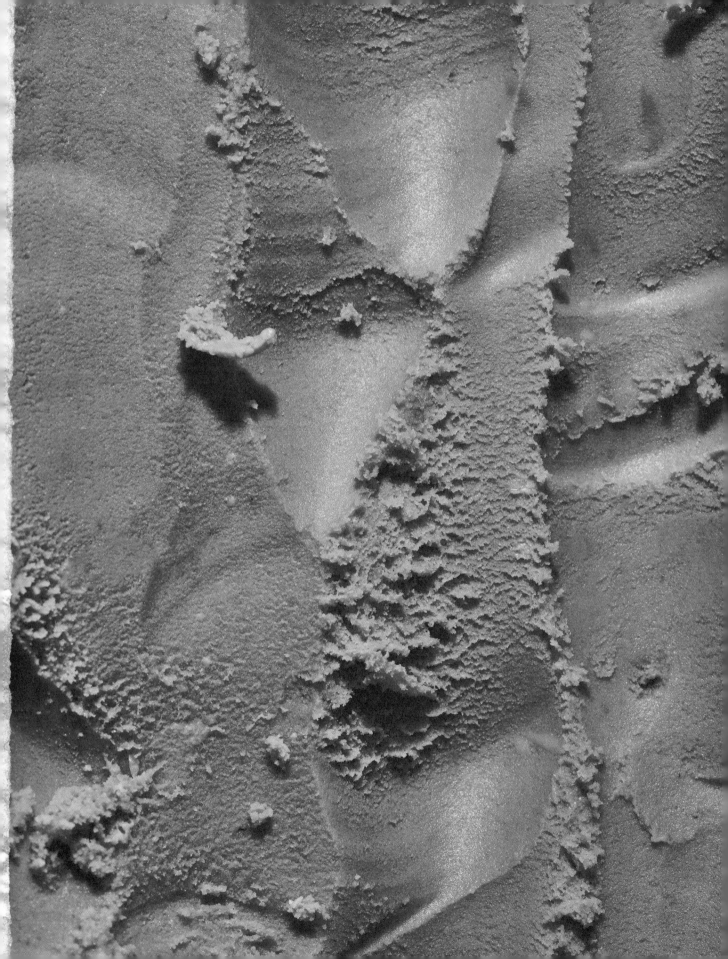